Living with Adversity

Living with Adversity

Eighteen Personal Accounts

Edited by
DAVID BENATAR

RESOURCE *Publications* · Eugene, Oregon

LIVING WITH ADVERSITY
Eighteen Personal Accounts

Copyright © 2026 Wipf and Stock Publishers. All rights reserved. Except for brief quotations in critical publications or reviews, no part of this book may be reproduced in any manner without prior written permission from the publisher. Write: Permissions, Wipf and Stock Publishers, 199 W. 8th Ave., Suite 3, Eugene, OR 97401.

Resource Publications
An Imprint of Wipf and Stock Publishers
199 W. 8th Ave., Suite 3
Eugene, OR 97401

www.wipfandstock.com

PAPERBACK ISBN: 979-8-3852-6670-8
HARDCOVER ISBN: 979-8-3852-6671-5
EBOOK ISBN: 979-8-3852-6672-2

VERSION NUMBER 010926

Dedicated to all the contributors,
one of whom is my father,
whose life with diabetes led me to conceive of this book.

Contents

Acknowledgements | ix
About the Contributors | xi

Introducing Adversity | 1
DAVID BENATAR

1. Living with Addiction | 14
   ROBERT KELLY

2. Living with the threat of Amyotrophic Lateral Sclerosis | 24
   ANITA C

3. Living with Cancer | 29
   PATTI WICKENS

4. Living with Complex Trauma | 38
   ANONYMOUS

5. Living with Diabetes | 46
   SOLOMON BENATAR

6. Living with Disfigurement | 55
   HENRIETTA ROSE-INNES

7. Living with Depression | 59
   ANTON FAGAN

8. Living with an Eating Disorder | 68
   ANNA REYKSÍK

9. Living with Hemophilia | 73
   JAN GLAZEWSKI

10. Living with Cluster Headaches | 84
    BOB WOLD

11. Living with a Heart Transplant | 91
    EVANCE KALULA

12. Living with (premature) Menopause | 99
    CANSU ÖZGE ÖZMEN

13. Living with Parkinson's Disease | 106
    DENIS DANEMAN

14. Living with Philosophical Isolation | 116
    AHMED

15. Living with Psychosis | 124
    ABIGAIL GOSSELIN

16. Living with Public Shame | 132
    REBECCA TUVEL

17. Living with one's child's Suicide| 142
    LYNNE KEETON

18. Swimming Against Adversity | 148
    ANTHONY S. REBUCK

Bibliography | 151

Acknowledgements

I AM GRATEFUL TO all the contributors to this volume for their willingness to share their experiences, their effort in writing their essays, and their patience in responding to my editorial suggestions.

Most of the contributing authors were previously known to me, either personally or via correspondence. However, my thanks go to those people who introduced me to others who have written an essay for this volume.

Finally, I thank members of my family for their interest in, and enthusiasm about this project, and for serving as sounding boards for many of the little decisions that had to be made on the long path from initial conception to publication.

About the Contributors

AHMED is a young Egyptian atheist, secular humanist, and software developer.

ANONYMOUS is a twenty-eight-year-old woman who lives in London, United Kingdom. She's a Software Engineering graduate who has worked in FinTech for six years but quit her corporate job last year in an attempt to escape the rat-race and to reevaluate her entire life.

DAVID BENATAR is Emeritus Professor of Philosophy at the University of Cape Town. His books include *Better Never to Have Been* (Oxford, 2006), *The Second Sexism* (Wiley-Blackwell, 2012), *The Human Predicament* (Oxford, 2017), and *Very Practical Ethics* (Oxford, 2024).

SOLOMON BENATAR is Emeritus Professor and former Head of Medicine at the University of Cape Town. His publications include *Global Health: Ethical Challenges*, co-edited with Gillian Brock (Cambridge, 2021).

ANITA C. is a nurse and a member of a family at significant elevated genetic risk of Amyotrophic Lateral Sclerosis.

DENIS DANEMAN is a seventy-five-year-old pediatric endocrinologist. His major area of medicine relates to the care of children with diabetes. He developed Parkinson's disease almost twenty years ago and continues to strive to maintain good health.

ANTON FAGAN is the former WP Schreiner Professor of Law at the University of Cape Town. His publications include *Undoing Delict: The South African Law of Delict under the Constitution* (Juta, 2018), and *Aquilian Liability in the South African Law of Delict* (Juta, 2019).

ABIGAIL GOSSELIN is Professor of Philosophy at Regis University in Denver, Colorado. She has published five books on philosophical issues related to mental illness, including *Mental Illness Stigma* (Cambridge, forthcoming) and *Mental Patient: Psychiatric Ethics from a Patient's Perspective* (MIT, 2022).

JAN I. GLAZEWSKI is Emeritus Professor at the Institute of Marine and Environmental Law at the University of Cape Town. Apart from academic publications, he has published a memoir, *Blood and Silver* (Tafelberg, 2022).

EVANCE KALULA is Emeritus Professor of Law, University of Cape Town, and Chairperson of the International Labour Organization Committee on Freedom of Association.

LYNNE D. KEETON is a retired private practise anaesthesiologist, and mother of two daughters.

ROBERT M. KELLY is Professor of Philosophy at Bakersfield College in California. His publications include "Towards a Dispositionalist (and Unifying) Account of Addiction," and "How an Addiction Ontology Can Unify Competing Conceptualizations of Addiction" (with Janna Hastings and Robert West).

CANSU ÖZGE ÖZMEN is Associate Professor of American Literature at Tekirdağ Namık Kemal University, Türkiye. Her research interests are Animal Studies, 19th-century travel literature, contemporary American fiction, and antinatalism.

ANTHONY REBUCK is a retired Professor of Medicine at the University of Toronto, and a specialist in respiratory diseases. He is the author of the book *Breathing Poison: Smoking, Pollution and the Haze*.

ANNA REYKSÍK is a *nom de plume* of a woman who has an eating disorder.

HENRIETTA ROSE-INNES is an author based in Cape Town. Her work, including the novels *Green Lion* and *Nineveh*, and several short story collections, has been widely published and translated. She has won the Caine Prize for African Writing and the University of Johannesburg Prize for translation.

REBECCA TUVEL is Associate Professor of Philosophy at Rhodes College. Her publications include "In Defense of Transracialism," "Putting the Appropriator Back in Cultural Appropriation," and "Against the Use of Knowledge Gained from Animal Experimentation."

PATTI WICKENS, ex-Environmental Principal for the De Beers Group, is now retired. She has a PhD in marine biology from the University of Cape Town.

About the Contributors

BOB WOLD is the founder and Executive Director of Clusterbusters, a nonprofit organization dedicated to research and advocacy to improve the lives of cluster headache patients.

Introducing Adversity

David Benatar

THE PERVASIVENESS OF ADVERSITY

Adversity is widespread. According to some views, it is so widespread that the phrase "Living with Adversity" is a redundancy. According to such views, to live *is* to face adversity—one cannot live without confronting adversity. Indeed, this (or something very close to it, namely Duḥkha) is, according to Buddhism, the first of the Four Noble Truths.[1]

One does not have to go this far to recognize that adversity is ubiquitous. For example, many people live with the adversity of destitution, disease, disability, or discrimination. However, considering *only* these conditions, underestimates how much adversity there is. First, not all forms of discrimination are recognized,[2] and some disabilities and diseases are "invisible"—to those not living with them. Second, and even more significant, there are many other kinds of adversity which are also invisible.

The recognition of this makes it clear why a common belief is false. That belief is that we can tell, by looking only at some limited categories, such as a person's race, class, sex, sexual orientation, and gender—and the intersection of them—whether a person faces adversity, and how much adversity they face.

We meet and interact with many people, but only rarely do we know anything about the hardships they face. When you look into the eyes of

---

1. The Buddhist claim is not the implausible one that the truths themselves are noble. Instead, they are noble truths because they are known to the noble one (Buddha) or to noble people (where "noble people" is obviously not a reference to social class).
2. Benatar, *The Second Sexism*.

another human, you might sometimes see their suffering. More often, however, you will not know what suffering is experienced in the brain behind those eyes. Somebody may appear well, happy, and successful. Yet, you do not know what past trauma they carry, what worries they have, or what physical or mental pain they experience.

There are many reasons why you will not know this. Our interactions with people are often fleeting. One sees the cashier in the checkout line in the grocery store, the bus driver as one boards a bus, or one interacts with the customer service representative when one calls a company. On these occasions our interaction is brief and must be focused. If, as one boarded the bus, the driver were to pour out his heart, the bus would not reach its destinations.

Nor is it only fleeting interactions that are superficial. You might have sustained interaction with your doctor, but it would be highly inappropriate for your doctor to tell you about his or her problems. The same is true of your teacher, your banker, or your accountant.

There are other social and psychological forces that also militate against your learning about others' adversities. For example, there is a powerful "positivity" imperative. When we ask, "How are you?", the last thing we typically want to hear, is a full disclosure of all the person's travails. Indeed, we do not even want a terse "Not good" because the only acceptable social response to such a reply (unlike a positive "All good"), is to invite the longer explanation that we often do not want.

We want people to present themselves as positive, and not only because negativity is much more time- and energy-consuming. Many people are in denial not only of death, as Ernest Becker noted,[3] but of the pervasiveness of suffering more generally. People do not like a "Debbie Downer,"[4] but are full of praise for positive people, and especially those who are positive in response to adversity. There are few, if any complaints, about somebody who is a "Chipper Charley"—a term I coin as an alliterative counterpart.[5]

Not all the pressure to be positive is externally generated. Some of the pressure comes from within the person facing adversity. This is because many adversities create a sense of vulnerability. Speaking about one's struggles and indignities, is also to expose one's vulnerability. This is perhaps best recognized among victims of rape and other sexual assault, and perhaps

---

3. Becker, *The Denial of Death*.
4. Wikipedia, "Debbie Downer."
5. A more common term is "Pollyanna."

slightly less so among those suffering from mental illness, as well as select physical conditions such as HIV. However, it applies more generally.

These feelings of vulnerability are complex. To some extent they can arise from a fear of stigma. This is often true in the case of mental illness, HIV, and also of rape and sexual assault in those societies in which victims are (inappropriately) blamed for their own victimization. Stigma, however, is not the only fear. Somebody might reasonably fear that their vulnerability will be exploited in some way.

There might also be a sense of shame—not in the sense of a moral failing, but rather in the same sense in which forced bodily exposure can cause the victim to feel shamed. The victim feels the indignity to which he or she has been subjected and does not wish to amplify this through disclosure of the indignity.

VARYING RESPONSES

There are thus many good reasons why people often do not speak about the adversities they are facing. This also explains why, in this volume, some contributors have written either under pseudonyms or anonymously, or in some other way that inhibits their being identified. Ahmed, for example, is the author of the chapter on living with "philosophical isolation." He is an atheist in an intolerant religious society, where being outed—or outing oneself—as an atheist carries the risk of serious social and even legal repercussions.

Other contributors to this book have been willing to identify themselves. These different preferences constitute evidence of individual variation, not only in circumstances, as well as the extent to which people put a premium on privacy, but also in how people cope with adversity. What is a reasonable disclosure for some people is too much (or too dangerous) for others. Similarly, for some people, it is empowering to provide, in a personally identifiable way, an account of what they face. Others are willing to provide an account, but do not want to be identifiable.

Yet others whom I approached to write, decided against doing so—some immediately in response to the invitation, and others after they tried to draft something. Their reasons also varied. Among those who attempted to draft a chapter, the most common explanation for their decision was that they could not find a way to express themselves without revealing more (about themselves or indirectly about others) than they were comfortable disclosing.

All these responses are entirely reasonable and understandable, even though they conflict with one another. This is because the aptness of a response is not determined only by the nature of the adversity, but also by the nature of the person living with it.

This is true even of the person who immediately refused an invitation to contribute a piece about his serious physical disability on the grounds that "plenty of people have suffered far worse things than I did," and that he intensely disliked people brandishing and almost boasting about their disability, "inviting people to marvel at their courage."

None of the contributors to this volume is guilty of this, thereby revealing that one can recount one's adversities without denying that others are worse off, and without seeking admiration. They write matter-of-factly and without self-pity. Nevertheless, the sensitivity of the person who declined to write is an understandable response to adversity.

Many of the contributors, along with some who attempted but eventually decided against contributing, expressed the view that writing the piece had been helpful to them. For many people there is some catharsis in putting into words, and especially writing, that which they experience.

This is one reason why I mostly invited people who had not written publicly about their condition. I wanted to provide a forum for those who had not previously had an opportunity to express themselves about their adversities.

AIM OF THE BOOK

While at least some of the authors might have benefited from providing an account of living with their respective adversities, the primary intended beneficiaries are the book's prospective readers rather than its authors.

The aim of the book is to provide an insight into the adversities of others, to expose what, for the reasons outlined earlier, is often hidden. The impetus for the collection is an adversity that I witnessed (rather than personally experienced)—namely, my father's living with type-1 diabetes, and all that that involves. It struck me that the challenges, hidden suffering, and adverse health effects of this condition are rarely appreciated by those who neither have diabetes nor are close to somebody who does.

It thus occurred to me that there would be value in a book that could introduce readers to a range of adversities and what it is like to live with them. I asked my father to write about his condition, and then proceeded to ask a range of others. Accumulating the essays in this book turned out to be a challenge.

The challenge was to find people living with adversities, who were willing to write about these, and who had the ability to write an account worthy of publication. Identifying people who met all these conditions, and then eliciting the papers, was a slow process. I am grateful to the early contributors for their patience while the later contributions were gradually collected.

Of course, there are already many essays and book-length accounts of living with different adversities—addiction,[6] cancer,[7] depression,[8] poverty,[9] and rape,[10] for example. The current volume is nonetheless distinctive because it draws together, in a single collection, essays on a broad range of adversities. This enables the reader to get a good sense of a variety of ways in which life throws up challenges for different people.

There is no way that a single volume of reasonable length could possibly cover the full range of adversities that people confront. Any endeavour to do that would have to reach encyclopedic proportions. What it gained in comprehensiveness, it would lose in readability and mental digestibility. Thus, choices had to be made. These were partly determined by which suitable contributors I could secure. However, I did also attempt to ensure some diversity of adversity—for example, both physical and mental challenges, and both medical and non-medical conditions.

Nevertheless, there is some value in indicating some of the hardships that were *not* included, as this will reinforce just how many adversities are possible. There are no entries on albinism, amputation, asthma, blindness, chronic fatigue syndrome (myalgic encephalomyelitis), Creutzfeldt–Jakob disease, cystic fibrosis, deafness, dementia, divorce, dwarfism, epilepsy, eczema (or psoriasis), homelessness, incarceration, incontinence, inflammatory bowel disease, loneliness, multiple sclerosis, obesity, obsessive compulsive disorder (OCD), paraplegia, poverty, rape or sexual assault, renal

---

6. Sheff, *Tweak*.
7. Rakoff, *When My World Was Small*.
8. Styron, *Darkness Visible*; Solomon, *The Noonday Demon*.
9. McCourt, *Angela's Ashes*; Walls, *The Class Castle*.
10. Estrich, *Real Rape*, 1–7.

failure, schizophrenia, social phobia, sleep disorder or deprivation, stroke, unemployment, war, or the uncertainty of living with an undiagnosed medical condition.

Some conditions not directly covered either receive mention in one of the essays or bear some resemblance to, or overlap with, conditions that are included. For example, there is no essay on sexually transmitted disease, but the chapter on hemophilia includes the non-sexual contraction of HIV through contaminated blood products. The chapter on hemophilia also includes discussion of resultant joint problems, which have some of the same effects on wellbeing as arthritis, which is not included. Menstrual problems are not covered in a separate essay, but menstruation is mentioned in the chapter on premature menopause.

Ideally, many of the contributing authors would have been people I did not already know—because the people I know are not representative of all humanity. However, it should not be surprising that my call for papers was more likely to reach people who, in some sense, were in my "orbit." One, as I have noted, is one of my parents. Others are friends and colleagues. Yet others entered my orbit through referral by people I already knew. A final category includes people who had contacted me about my work about the quality of life, and who I detected would be suitable contributors.

It was not likely that I would reach people who do not speak English, or people in impoverished countries who are so deprived that writing essays about poverty or other hardships would be the lowest of their priorities, even if, despite their deprived educational opportunities, they had the ability to write a publishable essay. I am acutely aware that the collection is consequently unrepresentative of human adversity globally. Wide swathes of Africa, Asia, Europe, Central and South America, for example, do not feature either at all or to the extent that they ideally should.

Nevertheless, the book's contributors include people from Canada, Egypt, South Africa (including one Zambian expat), Türkiye, the United Kingdom, and the United States of America. Moreover, some "comfort"—about the lack of representativity—should be derived from this fact: Just as I readily find adversity in my orbit, so anybody, anywhere, would readily find adversity in theirs. In that sense, my casting my net *is* representative. However, what is comforting about the representativity problem is the opposite—depressing—about the full scope of human-endured adversity. The adversity of the people I know is not an aberration. If anything, the total adversity of others is still worse.

The book focuses only on *human* adversities. This is not because the adversities of animals are unimportant. Quite the opposite. Animals—both wild, and those reared to provide food for humans—suffer unspeakably. Moreover, many humans are in even greater denial about animal suffering than they are about the suffering of their fellow humans.

While this is noteworthy, this book is not the place to showcase animal suffering. This is because the book is a collection of first-person accounts of living with adversity, which animals are unable to provide.

Prospective contributors to the book were asked to provide first-person essay-length narratives aimed at a general (rather than an academic) audience. They were thus asked to write in clear, accessible language, preferably without references and endnotes (or to keep references and endnotes to an absolute minimum). I asked authors to convey to those not living with a condition what it is like to live with it. I asked them to include factual details, as well as subjective experience of the condition—what it feels like, both physically and psychologically, to live with the condition. I said that they should convey the hardships and challenges of living with the condition, but that they should also include methods of adaptation or coping mechanisms. Where applicable, they should indicate any changes in these various matters either over time or over the course of the condition.

The authors were reassured that there was no obligation to "be positive"—that I was not seeking redemptive or pollyannaish narratives—but that the narratives should also not exaggerate the adversity. Some humour, I said, was welcome but not required.

OUTLINE

The resultant essays are gathered here. That there are eighteen of them is not entirely a coincidence. I had partially aimed at this number for playful reasons: "Gematria" is the practice of assigning a numerical value to each of the letters in the Hebrew alphabet, thus yielding a numerical value for each word.[11] The Hebrew word for the verb "live" (חי, *khai*) has a numerical value of eighteen.[12] In consequence, the number eighteen is seen as auspicious.

---

11. Gematria very likely had its roots in the more ancient practice, isopsephy, which assigned numerical value to each of the letters in the Greek alphabet.

12. A common mistake is to suggest that חי means "life", but the Hebrew word for "life" is חיים (*khayím*) which has a numerical value of sixty-eight.

By contrast, by including eighteen accounts of adversity, I mischievously allude to the inauspicious connection between living and adversity.

The adversities appear in roughly alphabetic order:

Living with Addiction

Robert Kelly, a philosopher, writes about his addiction. He has not had a drink since 26 May 2008, but he is unsure whether he is sober. This is because he takes his alcohol consumption to be but one manifestation of an underlying addiction. Other manifestations have been drugs, relationships, and even his professional activities. He writes about the varying impacts of these addictions on his wellbeing and the wellbeing of those close to him.

Living with the threat of Amyotrophic Lateral Sclerosis

This chapter is written by Anita C., who is both a nurse and a member of a family at significantly elevated genetic risk of Amyotrophic Lateral Sclerosis (ALS). She has cared for various members of her family who have died from the disease. She and her children live with the possibility that they too will be diagnosed with the condition. Given the familial nature of this disease, the author prefers not to be fully identified, in order not to indirectly breach the privacy of other members of her family.

Living with Cancer

In this chapter, Patti Wickens, a marine scientist who later became an environmental manager, provides a harrowing rollercoaster account of the horrors of living with, and surviving cancer—twice! She also explains the impact of these illnesses on her family. Her experience was exacerbated because she first became ill at the beginning of the COVID-19 pandemic, which added to the adversity.

Living with Complex Trauma

The anonymous author of this chapter describes her traumatic childhood in which her parents regularly fought. Her father controlled both her and her mother, and physically abused her mother. Yet her relationship with her father is not uncomplicated, because she recognizes that he also loves her deeply. The author was forced to grow up prematurely by comforting her mother and arbitrating between her parents. However, she has suffered psychologically. She lacks self-esteem, has had intrusive thoughts, regularly feels anger and anxiety, and considers suicide daily.

Living with Diabetes

The author of this chapter, Solomon Benatar, a retired professor of medicine, has lived with type-1 diabetes for nearly seventy years. He describes the myriad challenges of living with this condition, as well as the unfortunate sequelae, including coronary artery disease, and how it has enhanced his awareness of the hidden suffering of his patients. Given the length of time that he has been diabetic, he provides an interesting account of how living with diabetes has changed over time.

Living with Disfigurement

Henrietta Rose-Innes, the author of this chapter, is a writer, editor, and translator. She developed a facial cancer that required disfiguring surgery. She describes the difficulties of living with this disfigurement, how masks during the COVID-19 epidemic helped her, and how her disfigurement affected not only her speaking, but also her writing. This chapter is the first piece of creative writing she was able to write since the surgery.

Living with Depression

Anton Fagan, a now retired law professor, had an unexpected depressive episode. He writes candidly and engagingly about the experience, and about how he, with help of his wife and family, eventually found his way through the worst of it. He hopes that his wife is correct that it was a once-off event, but "the possibility that she might not be is a constant worry."

Living with an Eating Disorder

In this chapter, the author, writing under the pseudonym "Anna Reyksík," describes her long struggle with an eating disorder. Dissatisfied with her body weight, she starved herself. That relieved her body image dissatisfaction, but had adverse effects on her health, most importantly a lack of energy. She now eats more healthily, but part of her longs for her slimmer body.

Living with Hemophilia

Jan Glazewski is a retired professor of law. He was born with hemophilia. He nearly died as an infant, when he was circumcised. The doctor who performed the procedure had done so in the face of Jan's father's protestations, which were informed by the death of an elder son, Jan's older brother. Later in life, the need for intravenous transfusions of blood clotting products led to Jan's contracting HIV from a contaminated blood product. This was during the early years of awareness about this virus. Thus, he also describes living with HIV.

Living with Cluster Headaches

In this chapter, Bob Wold writes about the onset of cyclical unbearable headaches, the difficulty of living with a condition of unknown aetiology, how he was supported by his family and, after the development of the internet, an online community of fellow sufferers. He eventually founded Clusterbusters, a non-profit dedicated to research into the condition.

Living with a Heart Transplant

Evance Kalula, yet another retired law professor, grew up in a mining area in Zambia, where his father was an impoverished miner. The author's heart condition might be attributable to the smog generated by the smelters in the area. He avoided becoming a miner himself through his bookishness. He went to Oxford as a Rhodes Scholar. Eventually, however, he required a heart transplant, which he received in Cape Town, where he was then living and where the world's first heart transplant had been performed in 1967. He describes both his travails and the network of support that has helped him through these.

Living with (premature) Menopause

Cansu Özge Özmen is a professor of English. She writes about how, as an adolescent, she yearned to menstruate, like other girls in her class, but once menstruation began, she very rapidly resented it. Following treatment for cancer, she underwent surgery that thrust her, at age thirty-eight, into premature menopause. She describes the varied challenges that menopause in general, and surgically induced menopause in particular, poses. She notes that while she was a late bloomer, she became an early witherer.

Living with Parkinson's Disease

Denis Daneman, the author of this chapter, is a now retired medical professor who diagnosed his own Parkinson's Disease. He describes his initial reactions, how the disease has unfolded, how he has coped, and what he fears. He describes Parkinson's Disease not so much as a death sentence, but as a life sentence.

Living with Philosophical Isolation

Ahmed, the author of this chapter, is a young Egyptian atheist who needs to hide his views not only from the broader society but even from his immediate family. He fears legal repercussions from the state, and social and personal rejection by friends and family, if it were to be known that he is a "heretic." He writes good naturedly about the difficulties of having to hide such fundamental features of his worldview, but also how he copes with it.

Living with Psychosis

In this chapter, Abigail Gosselin, a philosophy professor, provides an account of living with an extended period of psychosis. She writes about the loss of her "I," of strange sensations and feelings, diminished comprehension, difficulties interacting with other people, having suicidal thoughts, and not only hearing voices in her head but also listening to them. She writes that her will and agency were superseded by the disease. She speaks of the many ways in which she became dependent on her husband. She eventually recovered, but fears a recurrence.

Living with Public Shame

Rebecca Tuvel is also a philosophy professor. She describes how she was subjected to a campaign of public shaming for having published an academic article, the content of which some of her fellow academics deemed unacceptable. She writes about her evolving reaction, her obsession with the controversy, the shame she felt, and also about the support she received. She now regards the "experience as the target of a massive online pile-on as one of the best things that ever happened" to her, "but also one of the worst."

Living with one's child's Suicide

Lynne Keeton is a medical doctor. Her chapter contains a moving account of her attempting to cope with the suicide of her daughter. She first describes her daughter's happy early childhood, and troubled adolescence and depression, and then discovering her daughter's lifeless body. Most of the chapter, however, is devoted to wrestling with the loss. She wants her daughter back but does not want to return her to the state of suffering that preceded her death.

Swimming Against Adversity

This concluding chapter is not focused on living with a particular adversity, but instead about one person's means of coping with adversities—by swimming. Anthony Rebuck, a retired doctor, has twice taken up swimming to counter adversity. The first adversity was antisemitism in the English boarding school to which he was sent (or, in his words, "sentenced"). The second adversity, six decades later, was cancer. He has literally swum against adversity. Others do so figuratively, with varying degrees of success.

OPTIMISM AND PESSIMISM

While all the contributors to this volume have faced adversity, they do not all have the same attitude towards it. Some are more optimistic and others more pessimistic. Both optimism and pessimism are a matter of degree. Moreover, both optimism and pessimism can be tensed. That is to say, one can be either optimistic or pessimistic about how well or badly things *have been*, *are*, or *will be*.

However, the applications of optimism and pessimism on which I wish to comment here are of a more general kind. What conclusions about life should we draw from the pervasiveness of adversity? Because my own views are more pessimistic, I should emphasise that many, but not all, of the contributing authors either do not share this pessimism or, at least, should not be assumed to share it.

My more pessimistic view, defended in other books[13] (and articles) is that life is so bad that it is always a serious harm to be brought into existence. This, I must immediately emphasize, does not imply that it is always (or even often) best to *cease* to exist. This is because both coming into existence and ceasing to exist are serious harms. I do not go so far as to say that suicide is *never* both rational and morally permissible. It *sometimes* is. However, I do not think that it is standardly a suitable response to the predicament of those who have already come into existence.

I happen to know that some of the contributing authors in this volume share my views about coming into existence, even when they do not make this clear in their contribution to this book. They include Ahmed, Cansu Özge Özmen, and the anonymous author of the chapter on living with complex trauma. Most of the others are silent on this topic or have a distinctly more optimistic view. For them, adversity, whether their own or somebody else's, is bad, but it is not bad enough to generate the conclusion that it would have been better if none of us had come into existence.

---

13. Benatar, *Better Never to Have Been*; Benatar and Wasserman, *Debating Procreation*; and Benatar, *The Human Predicament*.

1

Living with Addiction

Robert Kelly

I'M NOT AN ADDICT, MAYBE THAT'S A LIE

My last drink was on 26 May 2008. This was the night of my second *driving under the influence* (DUI), which totaled my car and nearly killed another driver. I had run a red light and smashed into their front driver's side wheel well, only a few feet from making direct contact with their door. After a handcuffed hospital stop and a night in the drunk tank, I had what seemed to me the more daunting task of facing my parents. In addition to being my second, this DUI followed almost a decade of progressively harmful drinking, the last few years adding harder drugs and being especially destructive. So, I was sure they would tell me they were fed up, that I was a fuck up, and offer a cynical "good luck" in dealing with the consequences and the rest of my life. When I got to their house the following morning, I was met with the opposite. My mom came outside, hugged me, and told me that *she* was sorry. We were both crying, and as confidently as I've ever said anything, I told her, "I'm never drinking again." I was four months passed twenty-three. Now at forty, I have never broken this promise.

Identifying as an addict has still always been confusing for me. I never "worked the steps" of Alcoholics Anonymous (AA), which starts with the confessional, "We admitted we were powerless over alcohol—that our lives had become unmanageable." I've only ever attended AA meetings a handful of times to help reduce my sentence after my second DUI. When I did go, I felt completely out of place. It was mostly rugged-looking men in their later forties and fifties who were as surprised as I was that a twenty-three-year-old kid was joining them declaring sobriety. I remember thinking how pathetic it was to be there. For them, I mean. They were the drunks, the alcoholics, the addicts. I was convinced I wasn't like them. An addict doesn't magically just decide to quit as I seemingly had. In my mind, I had been reckless at worst.

Denial is powerful, especially when giving it up requires admitting awful things about yourself. I denied that my drinking was problematic until it caused so much havoc that I could no longer convince myself that was true. Even when I quit, I still denied I was fundamentally the same as those alcoholics I'd met at AA. It was the sincerity of my promise to my mom that really did the heavy lifting in keeping me sober, which I have been for over seventeen years now.

Well, sort of. I did leave alcohol behind for good in May 2008, and cocaine about a year prior. However, cannabis and some psychedelics stayed on the menu for me, both early on in my sobriety and then making a comeback in the last few years. I sometimes think "sobriety" is more appropriate. My fellow west coast friends tell me that the proper vernacular for my proclivities is 'California sober'. If the Vans fit . . .

Much of this has made me wonder quite often whether I was ever truly addicted, rather than just an indulgent and care-free young person who liked partying. This has been an endless internal conflict for me that has long muddied my own understanding of my addiction, and myself, over the last twenty-five years or so. Thus, for me, living with addiction has been perennially intertwined with this confusion about exactly what and who I am. However, I've more recently come to see my addiction journey, my experience of it, and myself more clearly. My goal here is to tell that story.

BEEN THIS WAY SINCE EIGHTEEN

Actually, make that fourteen. I started drinking upon entering high school, as the world of raging hormones and insecurities was colliding with that of parties and more intensified peer pressure. Like most addictions, mine developed and progressed over time through continued behavioral patterns. Also, like most, it (or its severity) came and went at different points, and it showed itself in different forms. Alcohol use was the mainstay of my

Living with Adversity

addiction and its ensuing problems early on, but other behavioral patterns eventually stepped in to take the reins.

I used to see my addiction history as composed of two basic stages: drinking and sober. Of course, this was oversimplified because I was not *fully* sober after quitting drinking. In fact, I must admit that saying things like, "I've been sober for five years," often felt like lying. Counting from my alcohol sobriety was ignoring my subsequent use of other drugs. I used cannabis at least multiple times per week, often daily, from 2008 to 2011, and again since 2020, though now including occasional weeks-long breaks or spans of weekend-only use. My use of psychedelics—mostly mushrooms, sometimes ecstasy or "molly"—has been sparse, about two to three times a year during both of my "California sobriety" periods. Still, my addiction always felt centered on drinking, not drugs. How else did I try meth and crack *just once* without returning? How did I kick a year-long cocaine habit so abruptly and without treatment, and essentially on pain of shame and embarrassment from hearing "coke head" rumors about myself? How did I accomplish so much once drinking was eliminated, even if other drugs weren't? Because I was addicted to alcohol, I told myself.

I still feel a powerful sense that quitting drinking constitutes a stage-defining boundary in my addiction. Despite the psychedelics and cannabis through 2011, I had seriously "gotten my shit together" in a turn-your-life-around kind of way. From late high school until I quit drinking, my life was consumed by partying to get drunk. In fact, those years are so blurry that I had to reach out to family and long-time friends, and dig through old photos and social media accounts, to help piece things together. It didn't feel like such a mess at the time. Of course, there were signs, and I know I occasionally stopped to smell the fetid roses—*como la flor famosa de Selena, se habían marchitado* ("like Selena's famous flower, they had withered"). But humans are incredible adapters. Lie amongst wilting flowers long enough, I learned, and you just start getting used to the look (and smell) of things.

Examples of the drunken and destructive debauchery I got used to could easily exhaust this chapter. Many stories had to be told to me afterward, as blacking out was a regular occurrence for me, including while driving or waiting tables. Here is just one. I once blacked out at a neighboring Chili's after work, having arrived drunk via the car of a drunk stranger; not yet unusual, sadly. Sometime later, a family dining there came outside to find me passed out . . . in the backseat of their car! Apparently, a friend had arrived and found me lying in the grass near the parking lot just outside. My drunken gibberish led him to believe the nearby car, which happened to be unlocked, was mine. Luckily an employee I knew saw this scene unfolding and somehow got me into her car and out of there before the police arrived. I wish the story ended there. She dropped me off at my sister's apartment where I'd been living—how I will never know, given my inability to form coherent sentences. I then realized (or perhaps just thought) I didn't have my key and proceeded to kick the front door in before entering and passing out. I believe this was when my sister finally kicked me out, but neither she, my mom, nor I are exactly sure. The prevalence of such incidents, severity and all, made this unsurprising. And so, I had gotten used to things like disappointing people, ruining relationships, devaluing myself, and risking or losing whatever of value I had left—jobs, living arrangements, college, supportive friends and family, health, safety, freedom from jail. Above all, I had gotten used to the feeling of being barren of purpose and hope.

Quitting drinking in the wake of my second DUI genuinely changed much of this. Even then, the changes were not immediate because I had to detox and re-evaluate my life, both new undertakings for me at twenty-three. But I was soon back in college maintaining a 4.0 with a new sense of direction and inspiration in studying philosophy. Within a couple years, I was engaged to my live-in girlfriend and transferring to CSU Northridge in Los Angeles to finish my B.A. in philosophy. About two more years later, I was married, gearing up to graduate with honors, and moving to Buffalo to begin a fully funded Ph.D. in philosophy at SUNY Buffalo. I accomplished more than I ever thought I could after putting alcohol aside. Still, looking back I see a pyrrhic victory.

Despite full sobriety from 2011 to 2020, and its accompanying successes, my mental health and relationships, especially my marriage, struggled considerably. Moving to L.A. and then especially to Buffalo isolated my then wife and me from our family, friends, and most everything else familiar. Unfortunately, driven by my immaturity and complacency, I was largely unaware of this. Worse, I was selfishly and single-mindedly caught up in the idea that, after all, we were there for *me* and *my* goals. Rather than responding to the isolation and resulting vulnerability with efforts to re-establish trust and strengthen our relationship, I often whiffed at such opportunities; perhaps more often, I never even saw the pitch coming. Quite early on, this unfairly pitted my wife and marriage against philosophy and school in a battle for my attention—a battle that the former two lost decisively, I'm embarrassed to say. Importantly, this all unfolded progressively, without any substance use, and often in ways I am only privy to now with the benefit of hindsight, therapy, and significant personal growth, most of the latter occurring just in the six months or so leading up to my beginning to write this in mid-2024.

During my *fully* sober years, I had substituted drinking habits for philosophical pursuits; importantly, though, they served much the same purpose. More on this below. In January 2020, I moved home from Buffalo just over two months into my divorce and a year into a leave of absence from the PhD program. Shortly after my return, I again became *California* sober in more than just residence. Though I'd retuned to cannabis and psychedelics, I completed and defended my PhD within a year. However, my relationships continued to stumble. My relationship with my mom—the only family member I've ever communicated with regularly—gradually became comprised almost entirely of infrequent text messages, less frequent phone calls, and increasingly rarer visits. A romantic relationship I'd gotten into during my divorce fell apart midway through 2021. Then in January 2024, a second romantic relationship of over two years came to an end, and two almost 20-year friendships were strained to a halt. The timing was awful. A month prior I had moved into my own apartment, living on my own for the first time ever. It was the perfect storm for a plunge in mental health, and I experienced the darkest and loneliest months of my life.

Pulling out of that mental hell was incredibly difficult, but unimaginably rewarding. It forced some serious self-exploration, and I felt I was really starting to understand myself and my addiction in ways I don't think I would have otherwise. The connection between my substance abuse, my damaged relationships, and declining mental health became clearer. I started to see that my addiction was not to substances, and that it never really left, nor ever really changed. It only showed itself in different forms. After drinking, my pursuit of philosophy in my fully sober years and my pursuit of romantic relationships after my divorce most clearly constituted the newer manifestations of my addiction. Still, the underlying reason was always the same.

THESE ARE THE REASONS I DRINK

Alanis Morisette's song "Reasons I Drink" is one of several self-discovery anthems that helped dig me out of the mental rock bottom I had found myself in at the beginning of 2024. Feeling seen or, even better, understood, and knowing you're not alone in your experience are often helpful remedies when we're low. Solidarity in suffering is powerful, and for me at least, music became a ripe source of such healing. Like Morisette, I lied (often to myself) about being fine, sought comfort and reprieve from self-doubt, and battled internally with who and how I wanted to be. The song title is deceptive because, like me, Morisette believes her addiction goes much deeper than drinking. She alludes to work, food, and love addiction, and is, at bottom, really addressing her struggle with overdoing it generally. This was the struggle I was gaining clarity on for myself. I, too, had jumped from one consuming habit to another in terms of overt behaviors—alcohol, drugs, philosophy, relationships. These brought pleasure and masked pains, of course. But nothing gave me reprieve, nothing made my comfort so strong, like the feeling of acceptance and validation. I craved these feelings, and I craved connection to others as a way to secure them. This was *my* reason for overdoing it, and this validation-centered framing of my addiction helped explain and unify my personal narrative that has unfolded over the last twenty-five years or so.

Whatever the attachment, my addiction was always about systematically failing to control my desires. The behavior patterns I formed habitually resulted in harmful consequences that gave me plenty of sufficient reasons to stop or significantly modify them. Yet, I persisted. It took a long time to finally see it, but to me this disregard for all the good reasons around me to stop *was* my loss of control. I always thought an addiction should feel more... physical. Like a chemically driven attraction or "craving" towards a substance that I'd seen in movies like *Trainspotting, Basketball Diaries,* or *Leaving Las Vegas.* This is surely why I never suspected to admit I was addicted even in my fully sober years. It's surely why my addiction has been so bewildering to me, especially during my California sober years.

But shifting my focus to my insensitivity to the reasons that spoke against my behaviors, or spoke in favor of modifying them, has truly been enlightening. I didn't have to see my brain as "hijacked" by drugs, nor see myself as a robotic non-agent, to think I had lost control. My overdoing it became about my irrationality—my habitual failure to register the harmful consequences *as harmful,* as *reasons* for change, my failure to respond to those reasons if so registered, or both. These were the addiction-making features that spanned my addiction history independently of substance use, all along driven by my need, my craving, to be accepted and validated.

A salient illustration of this trend during my full sobriety was my pursuit of philosophy at what I retrospectively see as the expense of my marriage. The general theme, starting in my undergraduate years, was neglecting the needs of the latter to focus on the former. I don't mean that my failed marriage was *all* my fault or *solely* caused by this, but this value prioritization was certainly skewed and pivotal. For instance, I wouldn't have dared to reconsider my graduate school plans, nor my openness to location, despite the obvious difficulties for my wife regarding her job, routines, ties to family and friends, and so on. To be honest, I don't remember considering any of that at all. I hardly dared to miss a department talk to give *myself* some much-needed (and much-lacking) rest, let alone to spend some much-needed (and much-lacking) quality time with my then wife. Everything—my marriage, sleep, routines, mental resources—had to work around philosophy and school, which never turned off. This was personally exhausting, though I ignored it for quite a long time. Understandably, this also drained the life from my marriage, which ended as 2019 turned to 2020.

After my divorce and return home, my pursuit of romantic relationships is the most salient example. Consider that after ten years of my life with someone, the last seven married, I was in another committed relationship within two months of *moving out*, let alone being divorced. I even naively (to put it charitably) argued down the completely legitimate concerns she had about my readiness. This relationship ended after a year and a half. Within another two months, I did basically the same thing, only slightly more aware that I was not ready for it. Yet again, this didn't stop me. Instead, I insisted on a "situationship"—one foot in, one foot out—that I unfairly dragged out for years. As with my marriage, the cost in both cases was more than the failed relationship. My mental health suffered immensely through these years. This pattern was hardly a route to properly processing the devastation, loneliness, regret, shame, guilt, and other negative effects that loomed (and built) after moving back in with my parents as a divorced, jobless, thirty-five-year-old in existential crisis.

I also caused a lot of gratuitous suffering to people I still care for deeply; and I must admit while certainly not my intention, I was aware enough for the guilt I still feel to be completely apt. I felt my inability to fully commit in my post-divorce relationships. I sensed the difficulties and hurt this created on both sides. Deep down I knew I was doing something I shouldn't. Still, the fears of detaching were too much—of being left alone, failing at yet another relationship, admitting I had let my own comfort take priority over the obvious risk (and eventuality) of hurting someone I loved, and perhaps most of all, of being hated by them for having done so. Avoiding such things overshadowed my better sensibilities about what I was doing.

I've struggled with deep insecurities since my pre-teen years, mostly being obsessed with what others think of me. I am terrified of rejection and negative judgment, which surely drives my yearning for validation. I have no memory of ever *craving* a drink, by far the most serious of my substance issues, even after quitting. It was others' esteem and affection I was after. Most of this never went away. Realizing the true role this drive has played in my life is recent, allowing me to begin to work on mitigating both the feeling and its influence. But it was there all along, grounded in my lack of identity. I didn't know who I was or was supposed to be. I coped by trying to find the answer in others. Whatever they liked, whatever garnered their favorable attention, that's what I would do. That's who I would be.

This fueled my drinking in straightforward ways. High school is a bastion of peer pressure that feeds on the self-conscious and insecure. The restaurant industry is often no different. I became a sort of yes man, always afraid to disappoint. Sure, being drunk *chemically* reduced my inhibitions further, and regular drinking patterns became familiar and easy to maintain—humans are quite good at avoiding change. Yet the myopic pursuit of acceptance and approval was the lead foot on the accelerator that clouded all the reasons around me to say no. Getting sober only changed *what* I overdid and *who* it hurt. The cannabis helped maintain the feeling of acceptance and sense of identity, and it suffocated any day-to-day insecurities. By the time I had quit that, my philosophical pursuits were center stage. I became more consumed by approval (peers, professors, admissions committees, referees) and less sure of who and how I thought I should be. I again carved out any path to favorable attention, and I got lots of it in philosophy, even early on. Imposter syndrome in graduate school only stoked this fire.

My better judgment regarding who I was hurting, including myself, continued to be overshadowed. Like Morisette admits in her song, the behavioral grooves I had entrenched were so deep that I lost sight of where, or how, to draw the line. When my marriage ended, and my graduate career almost did, the pattern persisted. Across fourteen years, I spent no more than four months alone between my relationships; and not because I'm exceptionally good at healing from loss. The story is the same. I couldn't handle being alone in the trenches I dug out. The loss only fed my desire to feel I was still capable of being loved. It hurts to realize how hard my partners worked to ensure I felt that way, even when I clearly didn't deserve it—enter blinders and brand-new grooves for the same old habits.

And so it went for the reasons I drank, neglected my marriage for philosophy, and dove headfirst into relationships that I was incapable of giving sufficient effort and attention to. I was being completely irrational, so thirsty for being loved and accepted that I missed or was unmoved by good and fully visible reasons to stop or change—a hard swallow for a stubborn, self-critical philosopher.

SOMETIMES I FEEL LIKE I DON'T HAVE A PARTNER

I heard "Under the Bridge" by the Red Hot Chili Peppers a lot as a kid, but never grasped the deeper meaning until later experiencing what Anthony Kiedis, the group's lead singer, was expressing in his poem-turned-platinum-hit. His recounting of how it felt to be addicted is simultaneously beautiful and heartbreaking. His feeling of loneliness, and his fear of it, pour from the lyrics as if the song itself, as much as Kiedis, is crying for someone to listen. Like a Dostoevsky character, he finds companionship and understanding only in his city, Los Angeles. Her bridges may provide a stinging reminder of past attempts to achieve solace intravenously. Still, her hills, her breezes, and the familiarity she offers provide Kiedis the only comforting shoulder he has to cry on.

Kiedis also nicely conveys what I've been trying to get at in telling the story of how I have come to reinterpret my addiction narrative. Of course I had a drinking problem. But I couldn't understand why this meant I must be *addicted*. I was sure being an addict meant that things like choosing to quit and using drugs responsibly would've been impossible. I was *so* sure of this, that the subsequent fifteen "sober" years of harmful behavioral patterns never even registered as connected to that part of my life. Repeatedly, those closest to me significantly adjusted their relationship with me—regular avoidance, retracting trust, withdrawing emotionally, cutting ties altogether. I see now that they realized what I hadn't. My habits had got away from me in substantially harmful ways that disrupted my ability to be moved by good reasons. I cannot blame them for pulling back. Years of continually pointing out, explaining, avoiding, even managing someone's harmful behavior, especially as a victim of it, is surely as exhausting as it is unfair.

I finally feel that I see things more clearly now. Addiction is teeming with attachment issues. For me, and I think for Morisette and especially Kiedis, this was always about seeking validating human connection, love, and acceptance rather than regulating a chemical dependence. My addiction constituted an attempt to fill a space that, for different reasons through my life, felt void of those things. Understanding this has been pivotal in beginning to fill that void in healthier ways.

2

Living with the threat of Amyotrophic Lateral Sclerosis

Anita C

Amyotrophic Lateral Sclerosis. Also known as ALS or Lou Gehrig's Disease. I heard these words often when I was very young, but it had not affected anyone close to me, and so I really didn't know much about it. That is, until it did.

When I was fourteen years old, my mother started falling. She was getting weaker by the day. Ultimately, she was diagnosed with ALS at the age of thirty-five, and quickly needed total care. She initially had weakness in her legs. Due to a fall, she broke her leg and was then confined to a wheelchair. She was never able to walk again. She then developed upper body weakness and gradually arm weakness. She needed help with mobility, personal hygiene, feeding, and every day-to-day activity. My father and siblings were not able to handle the care my mom needed; so I did. I did the best job that a fourteen-year-old could. I helped her bathe, dress and move to the wheelchair. I did not understand ALS then. I asked my mom (through my tears) if the doctor could give her some of my muscles so she could be "OK." She did her best to explain it to me, but nothing helped. My mom prepared for her death by making charts to put up in the house for us kids, "how to do laundry," "how to cook certain foods," etc. I used those signs for a long time. And every time I looked at them, I thought of her and missed her.

My mom passed away five months later, after my first day of high school. My childhood ended that day. I had to be the responsible one. Cleaning, cooking, caring for my younger brother. And worrying. About everything. I became an angry teenager. I was mad "at God" for taking my mom and leaving me in this situation. This lasted for a few years and then I realized I needed to make something of my life and went to college to become a Registered Nurse. I think caring for my mother actually motivated me to pursue this profession.

At the time (1980) we did not know our family was affected by Familial ALS (FALS). Even though my mom was the twelfth person to die from it, we were told only that it had a "familial predisposition." We were told initially that it was not a genetic condition and not passed down amongst family members but that we were just "unlucky" in that multiple family members had it.

Eight years later, my mom's identical twin started having symptoms. She lived in Maryland. I took a leave of absence from my job as a nurse to help care for her. As they were identical twins, it was like watching my mom die all over again. She struggled with depression and fear. She had a nine-year-old daughter and knew she was not going to see her grow up. She progressed quickly and despite a tracheostomy and ventilator, she died nine months later.

I started having a recurring dream after my aunt died. It was my mom walking away from me. Her back was to me, and I was crying out to her. "Mom, please come back. I need you." I think this dream started because they were identical twins and the memories of my mom's death came back very strong after my aunt passed. To this day I still have that dream.

Our family then contacted a research team in Chicago, and had blood tests sent for everyone in the family who was willing to help. As I was a nurse, I went around and drew everyone's blood to send in. It was through this testing we found out that we had the SOD1 mutation. We always knew it was genetic, but now had confirmation. This information brought with it a different set of worries and concerns. Who was going to get it? When would it happen? And would we give it to our children. Over the next several years, a few cousins and my mom's older sister got ALS and quickly passed away.

Living with Adversity

In the mid 1990s I was working in the Pediatric ICU and during a code on a patient I could not lift an IV pump with my left arm. I had weakness and immediately thought "now I have it." I previously had decided not to find out my gene status. I was not ready mentally to have that information and deal with all the implications that it had. However, the weakness persisted for weeks so I finally got the courage to go to my family doctor. He convinced me to find out my gene status because "if I didn't have it, I was worrying for nothing."

He contacted Chicago, called me at home one evening, and told me I did, indeed, have the gene. I will never forget that call. The call that changed my life. I cried a lot. I went and had an EMG which showed I had a pinched nerve in my elbow. Now I had time. Time to live my life.

I went to graduate school and became a Pediatric Nurse Practitioner. I tried to forget about ALS; tried to put it out of my head. Sometimes successfully, sometimes not. But for the most part, I was able to function and thrive.

When I was thirty-two years old, I found out I was pregnant with twins. I was overjoyed at the news but at the same time my joy was overshadowed by the knowledge that they may have this gene. I can remember discussing with a friend that I don't regret my mom having me (despite the fact the ALS always overshadows everything), so I am going to enjoy the precious gifts I was given. My kids are the best thing that ever happened and are wonderful people.

For the next five or six years the twins and I lived our lives. We vacationed a lot—made as many memories as I could—and I was able to put ALS on the back burner. But as it always does, just when I was able to forget, it creeps back in. My older sister, who was thirty-nine developed symptoms. She was an advocate for ALS. She went to Washington and met with Hilary Clinton to reduce the waiting period for social security benefits for those diagnosed with ALS. But behind closed doors, she was not as strong. She was very emotional. She had two sons, nine- and thirteen-years old, and she spent a lot of her last days making them "memory boxes." I watched and wished she would have spent the time with them making memories instead of those boxes.

My sister lived in Michigan, and I left my young twins with my aunt so that I could go there and help my brother-in-law care for her. She died one year after diagnosis. I was broken-hearted for her boys as I knew exactly what they were feeling.

Anita C—Living with the threat of Amyotrophic Lateral Sclerosis

I struggled after my sister's death. I went to a counselor. I cried a lot. I would cry for no reason. I can laugh about it now, but I recall yelling at the kid in Tim Horton's drive-through because they didn't have a cinnamon raisin bagel. I cried for several minutes. But I knew it wasn't about the bagel. I just couldn't handle any more. I worried about leaving my young twins. I worried about them having the gene.

I decided I can't live like this. So, I sought help. I went to see a neurologist in my hometown, who basically told me I was going to die from ALS at some point, and so I should go enjoy my life. This answer was not acceptable. I needed to feel like I was doing something. I needed to help my family.

I contacted the Muscular Dystrophy Association, which gave me contact information for an ALS specialist in Syracuse (three hours' drive from my home). I went there and with the help of an amazingly compassionate physician, I began my involvement in FALS research. I started taking antioxidants and Riluzole, so I could feel as if I "was doing something." I got enrolled in the "*Pre-fALS*" research study (a study for people who are at risk for Familial ALS) and was more than willing to do anything to save my kids. I never thought this study would help me as I always felt I would get ALS as a young adult. However, I believed it might help my children's generation.

Again, I was able to move on, enjoy my kids and make memories. But I should have known better than to get comfortable. Now my younger brother is having leg weakness. He had not found out his gene status, and I always prayed he was the one who slipped through. But no. He was diagnosed at fifty-two. As he was not involved in the research, he had a delayed diagnosis and a delay in the experimental treatment that shows promise with our mutation. He has progressed and needs a feeding tube. He has a wife who does the physical care he needs, but I am called often to help him with the tube, feeds and to interpret medical information. I am no longer his sister. I am his medical liaison.

I also recently found out that all my nephews, my niece and my children have the mutation. Nobody has been spared. This brings many emotions. Guilt for passing it on. Survivors guilt for my siblings' struggles and that I don't have it—yet. And something I have never told my family, guilt for not wanting to go to them and help. As every time I watch another person die, I see my future.

I have tried to be open with my kids about FALS. I explained that knowledge is power and participating in the research gives you some feeling of control. Otherwise, there would be no control and living with this knowledge would be difficult, if not impossible.

3

Living with Cancer

Patti Wickens

It was in March 2020 that I was on a three-flight journey back home to Cape Town after a meeting in Lüderitz in Namibia and I was feeling really lousy. I popped paracetamols throughout the journey. This was the start of the COVID-19 pandemic but before lockdown. I just wanted to get home. Turns out I had mumps. However, I continued to feel awful, now with an accompanying pain in my abdomen and occasional vomiting. I saw my general practitioner (GP), who referred me to a specialist. Blood tests pointed to autoimmune pancreatitis that was treated with heavy doses of cortisone. But the symptoms continued. Scans, frequent blood tests and medical appointments followed, including a biopsy for a lump that appeared in the middle of my cheek, but fortunately that was benign.

Then one Saturday in early July the specialist called to say that my latest blood test showed signs of renal distress, and I should admit myself to hospital. I was there for two weeks under observation during which I lost weight. More biopsies were done of bone marrow, kidneys etc. I went into theatre and had a stent put into my bile duct. No visitors were allowed because of COVID-19 fears. So, I was alone in the room. I was feeling awful and just wanted to know what was wrong with me and how it could be fixed. One morning I got up and out of bed, only to find myself on the floor. I had become very weak and from then on, I was wheelchair-bound.

Then the bombshell... non-Hodgkins B-cell follicular lymphoma affecting my abdominal organs. But now my illness had a name! Because of the diagnosis, my family was allowed in to see me—so hard for them. Then I was allowed home for a few days. I still remember an outing to Blouberg, and being pushed along the promenade in a wheelchair. It was a beautiful day.

I saw the oncologist at the end of July and had to start chemotherapy the next day. This was to be the first of six treatments over the next four months. The first treatment was daunting but later it was to become routine. I would arrive at around 8 a.m., have blood tests done by one of the two very friendly sisters. They would chat to my husband, Geoff, joking that he was my PA because he would wheel me in, and be back later to wheel me out. Then I would be admitted to the ward for the day and get hooked up to the drip to start the R-CHOP chemotherapy infusion which would last until mid-afternoon. Then back home again. By mid-August my hair had thinned to the point that warranted shaving off the rest. As my daughter, Jamie (then nineteen), shaved off my hair, tears were flowing, but in the scheme of things this was really of no consequence. I was surprised by my response.

It was always grounding to see others in the Sunflower Ward who were having different types of chemotherapy—some looking quite well and others sickly. One day the person opposite me started talking to me, and we realised we had a mutual friend. So, it was a pleasant morning chatting. She had two types of cancer, and the chemotherapy didn't seem to be working. She left before me and went home to rest before heading out for radiation later that day. She looked well enough. It was a shock when about two weeks later I heard that she had died. Such is the nature of illness and life, and death—here today and gone tomorrow.

I would feel fine until about four days later when fatigue, nausea, vomiting, diarrhoea, and awful mouth ulcers would set in. There was always pain coupled with anxiety. Everything has medication to assist, but every medication also has side effects. What helps for pain may also cause nausea, etc. I found food overwhelming, but Geoff would kindly make something I felt I could eat, and would say "eat what you can and leave what you can't." This took the pressure off me.

Day nine or ten would be the low point, when my white blood cells would be almost non-existent. Then I would have abdomen injections of neupogen to help improve my white blood cell count. I needed to monitor any temperature spikes which would tell if there was an infection. This then required being admitted and put onto intravenous anti-biotics for five days. The hospital routine was blood tests at about 5 a.m., medication, blood pressure and blood glucose counts every few hours. I really disliked these stays because I struggled with eating and dreaded seeing the all too familiar dark blue lid over a meal. After a couple of days, I generally started to feel better but had to stay to the end of the antibiotic treatment.

On one occasion I felt very depressed and tearful. The counsellor was called, and her simple explanation was that I was physically feeling down because of the low resistance from an almost non-existence of white blood cells. This made me feel better, knowing it would change as the count picked up.

After one of the courses of chemotherapy I was sitting in my wheelchair outside at home and was slumped over. Geoff fortunately saw the signs and rushed me to the emergency room where I was admitted with dehydration and renal failure. I then had to stay in isolation for two weeks but was quite out of it for much of the time. There were always the endless beeping of a monitor and the extra beeping sound of a drip bag nearing completion. I became diabetic and so had to be careful with my diet and get used to having insulin injections into my abdomen. I often needed medication for anxiety. Luckily, I was on the hospital ground floor so my family could visit by standing outside the window and we could talk over a WhatsApp call. That made a huge difference.

By now I had lost about 30 kg which was 40 percent of my body weight. I hovered around 45 kgs and was still only able to walk with assistance. Geoff had moved our bed into the lounge so that when I was at home I could always be where the family was gathered, which was wonderful. With COVID-19 still restricting schooling and university on-site participation, both Asa (then ten) and Jamie were at home, as was Geoff, who had retired at the end of 2019 and now found he was automatically in a role of full-time caregiver, along with Jamie. They did this brilliantly.

Asa found my illness particularly hard. We had fostered him from a Place of Safety where he was placed soon after he was born because his mother was ill and could not look after him. This was not a planned move but sometimes one goes with the heart. When Jamie was nine, she asked if she could take a child from a home for an outing as her birthday gift. We started volunteering at this Place of Safety and met this tiny baby. Over time he and Jamie, in particular, had a real connection. After many months

Jamie was offered the opportunity of taking little Asa out for an afternoon. And the rest is another story. He is now our son. Asa went into denial about my illness and when asked about me, he would always say that I was fine. It was very hard for a young child to cope, and thus Jamie took him to play therapy, and eventually we all went and learnt a lot about coping

I realised just how much illness in the family affects so many people. While I was just trying to cope with feeling awful and the effects of treatment, my family was trying to cope with normal life and the worry that comes with having a patient at home. Sometimes, during a chemotherapy cycle, I would go into the hospital for regular blood tests and end up staying in hospital overnight for something like a blood transfusion. On other occasions, when my white cell count was low and there was the possibility of infection, I would be admitted and absent from home for a week. This was a very uncertain, unpredictable time for all. But there were also joyful times that really keep one going. Our first grandchild, Jude, was born in South Korea to our older daughter, Alex, in November 2020. Such excitement to lift everyone's spirits.

Friends and colleagues were incredible. The value that support provides is immeasurable. I was no longer at work but fully supported by the company I worked for. Our housekeeper would not go on leave because she felt she needed to help, especially with making sure everything was sterile, which was an amazing commitment. Although it was only just over four months of treatment, the latter part of the marathon seemed endless. I have to be honest that this was a very challenging journey for me and my family through much of the year 2020, but the end of the cancer treatment seemed in sight. I looked forward to Christmas when the chemicals would have been flushed from my body, and pain and nausea gone. Then all effort could be put into padding out my skeletal 45 kg frame. Progress was slow but it was a joy as I became no longer completely wheelchair-bound and could walk with assistance. This was immensely satisfying, even if super-slow.

I had a mascot accompany me all the time—Jamie's soft toy, Penelope, which is a grey manatee she had picked up in Florida earlier in 2020. Penny was on my bed wherever I was, and she was the connection to my family. Jamie's idea was that we have matching manatee tattoos done, when my skin is up to it. While I am not your typical person for tattoos, Jamie and I already have tattoos of semi-colons, in recognition of people suffering from depression, something Jamie has suffered with since high school, following the suicide of a friend. The meaning of the semi-colon is about affirmation and solidarity that suicide, depression and other mental health issues do not need to be the end. Also, that life can carry on after cancer (the semi-colon representing that the sentence has not finished).

I had led a hectically busy life, working with lots of associated travel, always with tremendous support at home. Looking after my health was on the backburner. But nothing hits home like one's health being directly affected and the breadth of that effect on others, especially one's family. I am eternally grateful to my family for caring for me "24/7" and for all the messages of support and wishes from colleagues and friends. One colleague was seconded into my work role and did my job for six months. In addition, she would send a motivational quote and beautiful pictures from the Namibian desert every single day. The quote I found the best was "When you come to the end of your rope, tie a knot and hang on"—Franklin D. Roosevelt. A few times I felt as though I could just slip away because I had come to the end of the rope. I needed to hold onto that knot.

After Christmas 2020, I was recovering and then went for a PET scan of my abdomen to see if any signs of the cancer remained. It was a tense wait for the call from the oncologist the next day. But the results of this scan showed I was clear! Two friends arrived one afternoon and did an impromptu "show" with placards, each with some words of encouragement. It was so special! I should have been happy, but I had a nagging feeling and remember saying to someone that I just don't feel joy like I think I should. The "broken me" had not yet become the "normal me." I suffered from neuropathy (numb feet and fingers)—still do—and had painful legs that would kick involuntarily, especially at night.

Overwhelmingly, I had an awful and constant headache. I went back and forth to the oncologist, GP, physiotherapist, and acupuncturist, but nothing helped. One day a friend came to massage my feet, which she would often kindly do, as would Jamie and Geoff. It really helped. She said she would massage my head gently and while doing so her words were "your head seems very busy." That should have been a telling sign.

My GP recommended a brain MRI, which was slotted in early one evening in February. My fear of the claustrophobia that was involved in having a brain scan, lying absolutely still, with a mask over my face and inside the noisy MRI machine for about forty-five minutes, was now of least concern to me. I kept my eyes closed throughout. The oncologist attended the scan. As I came out of the change room, he was there, and I could tell by his face that all was not right. He said it would need to be confirmed by the radiologist's review of the scan, but there was dense material where the brain tissue should have been. His words were a blur, and he kindly walked me out of the hospital. The next morning the oncologist showed us the brain scan. It was a brain tumor – a right occipital lesion. This confirmed the reason for my headache. Again, while daunting, at least my pain had a root cause.

Then was the awful task of telling Jamie. The father of Jamie's great childhood friend had died late the year before from a brain tumor. Trying to be convincing that this was different perhaps rang a bit hollow. She fetched Asa from school and told him. He just wanted to know if I would be at home, but unfortunately, I would be in hospital again. The previous six months had been so challenging with Jamie taking on the role of mom in my absence and we thought we had come to the end of the journey, but another one was just starting.

I had a lumbar puncture, with the first of the chemotherapy treatment injected into my spine. I then went into theatre to have a chest port fitted to enable easier administering of the strong chemotherapy treatment that was to come. It was Friday and I was allowed home for the weekend with cortisone for the pain and inflammation. I saw the oncologist on Monday morning after blood tests by the ever-friendly sisters. It may have been my imagination, but I felt like everyone I saw was treating me cautiously, which worried me. I asked the oncologist's receptionist about it, and she said it was just that they did not expect to see me back so soon after having been cleared. But the PET scan only covers the abdominal area so would not have picked up the brain tumor. That made me feel better and not like my condition was much worse than I thought, although I realized it was pretty bad.

On Tuesday, once my medical aid authorization had come through, I was admitted to the "non-tested" COVID-19 ward while I waited for the results of my COVID-19 test to come back. By the morning, I was back in the familiar Sunflower Ward, which was comforting. In the afternoon I went into theatre again to have my bile stent replaced. The next day the chemotherapy treatment started, now administered through the port on my chest. This was so much better than a drip in the arm. My arms had taken a hammering with the blood transfusions, chemotherapy treatment and hydration IVs. I was not feeling good, the headache persisted, and I was sensitive to light. My days were spent in a darkened room.

The chemotherapy treatment only lasted three days and then we waited for the side effects. I got used to maneuvering everywhere while attached to the IV line. Unplug the power, hold on to the drip stand, and go to the loo or go down the passage for a walk. My routine walk was through the Sunflower Ward, out into the passage, stop near the door to the garden to see some greenery and then on through to the other side of the hospital, near Radiology, and back. All the time I would be trolleying my drip stand that had a brown bag over the IV bag marked in bold red letters "Warning cytotoxic. Follow Safety precautions." This was what was being drained into me through my chest!

A week after the chemotherapy infusion had finished, I started vomiting and was in pain and with nausea all the time, alleviated by a range of medications, but never gone. I was on morphine for pain but that caused awful hallucinations. One night I phoned Geoff and asked him to help get all of the people out of my room because they were making such a noise! It was amusing in hindsight but scary at the time. I used to walk twice a day until my body weight had dropped too low—42 kg. I was then not allowed to use up any unnecessary calories. I had an inflatable mattress that moved gently all the time because I was not to move by myself. My mouth and throat were covered in ulcers, and my face so swollen that I couldn't speak. I was fed through my chest port because I couldn't eat, but I also desperately needed to maintain body weight.

The nursing staff—day and night—were absolutely brilliant. These sisters, nurses, and carers were my hospital family and a truly close-knit one. I had visits from the counsellor to help me cope. I was used to being organized and planning, but here there was much uncertainty about the specific path ahead. The dietician and the hospital caterer visited to discuss any kind of food that I may be able to get down. They said that I should not be too hard on myself about eating, and that I should just try soup. That was a relief, and I could get it down—first just clear soup and then thicker soup.

I would determinedly take medication for pain and nausea and then half an hour later, down the Fortisip—"a meal in a bottle." I really disliked them, as I did the "fat shots" that I had to down as well—a thick milky liquid in a small glass. I would try to take four to five of the former and three of the latter each day. Slowly my mouth improved. My daily bed bath was lovely, even with the red bio scrub liquid soap, and the kind nurses who took it all in their stride as they changed me and washed me top to toe. Soon I was out of nappies and could walk the short distance in my room to the loo. Then one day I was able to take a shower under the watchful eye of nurse. It was really wonderful!

Asa couldn't bear to come to the hospital, which was quite understandable, but Geoff and Jamie and friends used to call and visit often, which was so uplifting. These were window visits but sometimes indoor visits during which they had to wear an apron, gloves, and a mask because infection was such a real risk. I was very weak but would ask to be moved to a comfy chair and sit for an hour a day if I could manage that. Lying down was always preferable but even that was not always comfortable. In the evenings Geoff and I would do crosswords over the phone if we both were not too tired. After what seemed a long time, but in reality was only four weeks, it was agreed that I could go home. That morning, after having prepared myself mentally, the porter arrived and said I was going for x-rays. I just burst into tears. I was comforted by the staff, who said it was just to check that my bile stent was still good and that I was going home.

It was so good to be back home, but the reality was that looking after me was not plain sailing. Although they did it willingly, Geoff and Jamie had to be the sister, nurse, caterer, and carer. I would get very cold and would always be wrapped up and trying to keep warm. I still had a terrible ongoing headache and was on cortisone and heavy painkillers. Sometimes I would be crying in pain, holding onto Geoff until the pain killers took hold. I had to take these tablets every four hours and needed help with that. Geoff would wake up half an hour before, give me anti-nausea medication, and then half an hour later I could manage to take the pain killers. This regime was too exhausting, even with Jamie filling in every so often. It was fine for me because I could rest all day. But at home there was Asa to get to school and back, and home chores to be done.

It took some time but then I was ready to start radiotherapy. The first step was mapping the tumor so that the three radiation beams could be accurately positioned to target the tumor as best possible. Another MRI showed that in the seven and a half weeks since the first scan, the tumor had grown from 2,6 cm to 3,9 cm. It was no wonder I had such a terrible headache! Radiation was done as an outpatient five days a week for four weeks. The treatment involved wearing a molded hard plastic mask over my face, which was then clipped to the bed to keep my head absolutely still and in the same position every time. The radiation itself was a painless process lasting about half an hour but in the beginning, I would feel nauseous at the thought of it. The staff were amazing, and I would be wheeled back out to the waiting room, and another patient would go first, while an anti-nausea tablet worked. After about two weeks, my hair suddenly fell out in chunks and so it was time again to shave it all off. By this time the intense headache had subsided, and so I was feeling good.

By the end of the radiation treatment, my acute and peripheral eyesight were compromised, as was my hearing. My acute sight returned after some weeks, but the peripheral vision took longer. The latter meant no driving. Although I had not been able to drive for almost two years, it was a big blow to me to have lost my independence to some degree. But almost a year later my vision improved, and I have been able to drive. So empowering! I have hearing aids because my hearing is still not good and these help to make experiences more inclusive.

I was treated for post-traumatic stress because I became constantly overwhelmed by anxiety. Over the next year I completed my four maintenance treatments (of monoclonal antibodies that target cancer cells). It may sound odd, but I looked forward to going in and seeing the staff in the Sunflower Ward. They are so welcoming, remembering how ill I was, how my mobility has improved, and how my physical appearance changed—now with flesh on my bones and color in my cheeks. It is really affirming to see these wonderful people who helped me make it through.

Now Jamie and I have our matching tattoos of manatees . . .

4

Living with Complex Trauma

Anonymous

My parents fought a lot. Two days wouldn't go by without a fight at home. When I was four, I remember sitting on the edge of the bed, watching my parents argue. My mum was in hysterics and yanking an ironing cord round her neck. When I was five, my dad didn't like the shorts I wore and wanted me to change. I said no, and so he screamed at me whilst pulling my arm to express his disapproval. I wet myself because I was so scared, and had to change the shorts anyway. He looked at me with disgust. I've seen my father repeatedly slap my mother with a pack of files whilst she sat on a sofa like a deer caught in headlights. I've seen him shove rice into my mum's mouth because he didn't like how it was prepared. I've seen him draw a knife out of a drawer threatening to kill himself. I've seen residual blood on the fireplace, where my mum repeatedly banged her head because she couldn't take it anymore. The list goes on.

My dad was physically and emotionally abusive, and my mum would self-harm. My dad was also very controlling. He controlled how I spoke, walked, ate, dressed, and practically anything that did not align with his fickle expectations. If my mother and I re-wore a coat or an article of clothing he was not fond of, there would be no leaving the house till that was changed. Everything was catered to my father's mood swings. Should anything challenge that, we had to be prepared for war. I, since a young age, advised my mother to divorce, but it was something she couldn't do. Part of me still resents her for that.

My dad had anger issues, and no amount of sense would calm him down. My father has the capacity to drive any human insane. Truly. He'd drive my mum up the wall. Out of desperation, she would self-harm as an indication for him to stop whatever it was he was saying. Only then, would he ease off. Not long ago my dad called me for help during a family holiday because my mum was hitting herself with a brick during an argument. Once again, he probably enraged her. He called her "crazy." He did not consider for a moment that he probably had a part to play. Boundaries do not exist in my family. I can't guarantee that I wouldn't have killed him if I did not fear imprisonment for doing so.

The absurdity is that my father loves me very deeply and will do anything for me. This is what I struggle with the most. I write this essay with great guilt, as there's probably no one in this world who will ever love me as much as he does. How can a person who caused so much pain, be so caring and generous? Had he consistently caused harm, at least my brain could process it and shun him. Alas, due to his positive attributes I experience this confusion every day.

I had to become an adult while I was still a child, because I was performing roles that were not a child's responsibility. Being an only child only exacerbated matters. I would patiently try to explain to my father that there was no need to get angry, that he could talk to me and my mum in a gentle tone and how we would still listen.

During arguments my mother and father would involve me, asking me to pick who was right or wrong, both desperately explaining their sides of the story hoping my verdict was in their favour. I often favoured and defended my mum fiercely. However, my mother wasn't allowed to participate in arguments between my father and me. If she would speak up, my dad would snap at her, yelling "why are you getting involved?" I hated him for this. How could a mother not be allowed to defend her own child? He would shut her up so awfully that, as I got older, I *instantly* told my mother to shush the second she spoke up. This was to spare her any verbal abuse from my father.

Another way that I, the child, was forced to become the parent was that I would comfort my mother each time she was hurt, telling her everything would be okay, that she had me, and how there was a solution to everything. That's probably why she confided in me sometimes. I was mature for my age, after all.

There's this one jarring memory that still stays with me from when I was a teen: I did not witness my dad hitting my mum on this occasion, but shortly afterwards she confided in me tearfully, saying "He hit me a lot this time." It was something that I had never heard from her. She's stoical, and thus for her to say, "a lot," it must have been really a lot. I hugged her and let her sob on my shoulder.

I have another memory from when I was six or seven years old, having a bath. I heard commotion and so I stepped out of the bath and peaked through the bathroom door. I saw my mother kneeled, sobbing next to the stairs; her head rested on the baluster. I walked out and squatted down beside her, naked. I weaved my arm into hers and rested my head on her shoulder and stroked her arm whilst she wept. My dad was standing upright screaming at her, motioning his hands, he stormed off shortly after I arrived.

My mother and I once went to a local park after another fight at home. It was autumn, and I used to love jumping in the crisp leaves. I was very young and innocent; I was convinced that my mother and I could build a little hut out of twigs, with a roof covered with dried leaves, and live in the park, safe and sound. We didn't have to go home. We didn't need anyone else.

Considering the history of abuse, I never felt safe around my father, even when he did no harm and just wanted to see how I was doing. When my father would return from late shifts, the second I heard the key enter the door lock, my heart would race. I would pretend to be asleep. If I had to go to the bathroom, I would avoid doing so until he went to bed. His presence in the house sent me into panic. I felt guilty and mean, but how else could I feel safe? I just wanted to be alone in my room. I cannot relax around him, even now. Once I was asleep, I would experience nightmares often, and would yell. My mother would come rushing afterwards to pacify me, and sleep with me till the next morning.

I get triggered very easily. A few days ago, my parents were on holiday, and my mother sent a harmless photo of them posing happily next to a statue. I immediately recognised that she was wearing a shirt that was of a cut that she would never have picked. It was my father's choice. Still, I knew she wore it anyway to make him happy. I felt extreme disgust and had flashbacks of how, during my upbringing, we were controlled on what we were permitted and not permitted to wear.

That night, I attempted for hours to sleep and distract myself, but I failed. I was hot and sweaty, and my mind was racing. I felt incredible rage and wanted to stop feeling so furious at how he still had an influence over us. I had an overwhelming urge, not out of sadness but pure rage, to go to the kitchen drawer, grab a knife and cut an artery. Self-harm need not be pathetic. It can be violence that you direct towards yourself because you cannot direct it at someone else. I felt repulsed at my mother for tolerating such a man.

I desperately called her at 3:30 a.m. to express how I felt. I wailed at how unacceptable it was. Begging her to come back home and not bring him. Once it was off my chest, I felt somewhat better. The next day was my dad's birthday. I wished him, and the three of us had a very pleasant conversation. It's confounding how we can jump between having the most harrowing interactions to the most wholesome ones. It's unsettling how erratic my family dynamics can be. It makes no sense. I've spent years trying to understand it, and failed. Lately I've found some solace in not worrying about labelling our family relationship as "good" nor "bad." It helps to not be wound up by the need to classify it.

I don't have a sense of self-esteem, I have "other-esteem," as my self-worth has always been dependent on external validation. My target has been either to impress others via my looks or achievements. A consequence was that hobbies were never hobbies. They were instead a chore and source of stress when I wasn't the "best." Being able to do things just for the sake of it, or out of pure joy without judgement, is a new concept to me.

Moreover, I'm averse to doing things slowly. If I take longer than I should to finish something, I feel worthless. Society rewards speedy results. I was praised for being mature for my age and accomplishing things young. Given that I am now approaching my thirties, there are fewer things that I can realistically do whilst still being considered objectively "young." As insane as it may sound, I feel awfully disappointed with myself, as I won't be able to retire by the age of thirty. The degree to which I chastise myself for not achieving something by some arbitrary age is foolish.

It's very challenging when achievements are tied so heavily to age; it becomes part of your identity. Birthdays terrify me. I remember being twenty-two and deciding that I wanted to die at the age of thirty-six, as I genuinely could not understand the point of living beyond that age. After all, that was the age at which Marilyn Monroe passed away.

I used to struggle horribly with intrusive thoughts. One of the worst periods I experienced of this was during secondary school, in Year Seven. Out of the blue, my mind started tormenting me with intrusive thoughts surrounding a mathematics teacher of mine.

The intrusive thoughts were of a sexual nature that made me feel so repulsed by him. Nothing helped me shake those thoughts. Constantly my mind formed unwelcomed images of him making advances towards me. I was never more disgusted by a person in my life. To make matters worse, my brain kept creating ridiculous connections between me and him: "What if he took the same bus home as I did?" "What if he sat on the same chair as mine?" "What if he liked the same food as me?" "What if he stepped on the same stone as I did just now?" "What if he liked me?!" I wanted to have no link to him whatsoever. If I could change planets, I would have. Everything I did or thought, my brain used that to form some absurd connection between me and him. Every waking moment was about that. It was nine months of hell.

My life's sole focus became to create as much distance from him as possible, and to avoid him at all costs. When he wrote on the whiteboard and I thought his handwriting looked like mine, I changed the way I wrote. If he borrowed my chair, I swapped it. If he used a pen of mine, I threw it away. If he were walking out of the classroom door when I happened to be in the corridor, I ran. Coincidentally, my cat's vet used to be in the same area where he lived, I avoided going there too. I was scared even to breathe the air around him.

It was completely nonsensical, as he did absolutely nothing to hurt me. Unsure what the trigger was, but I felt disgust to such an intense degree that I switched overnight from being this teacher's pet to despising him. It shows how obsessive-compulsive thoughts can spiral and avalanche in one's mind.

I am hypervigilant and I hate loud, unexpected noises. I'm allergic to uncertainty and should I be waiting on any news, I imagine the worst. Whilst shopping as a teen, I would simply walk out the second a song came on that I did not fancy. The song would invoke certain emotions in me, reminding me of sad memories, and I did not have the mental bandwidth to tolerate it. I hated R&B, and still detest euphoric "uplifting" music.

Most of my waking moments are either in anger or anxiety. Often when I feel anger, even over the most mundane of things, such as washing the dishes, my immediate urge is to shoot myself in the head or hang myself. Suicidal ideation has become a permanent resident in my "self-help" tool kit. It is the first solution my mind resorts to when I face any hardship, no matter how big or small.

Dialectical Behavioural Therapy (DBT) taught me that each emotion we feel has a unique underlying message that's being signalled to us. Unfortunately, often for people with trauma or personality disorders, emotional urges are unjustifiably strong and heavily conceal this deeper message. We tend to act on urges as opposed to recognising why we are feeling a certain emotion. For example, the underlying message for anger is for something to stop or change. Despite knowing this, I still struggle to feel appropriate levels of anger even though I know how ridiculous it is wanting to die over a tough grease stain.

Things that an average person doesn't notice, I pick up on immediately. The world is my trigger: I overthink everything, whether it's because a neighbour didn't say "Hello" in their usual lilt, or falling into nervous breakdown just because my manager was typing at his keyboard loudly. My brain is a broken threat detection machine which latches onto something even though logically there is no need to. It sometimes does this as a delayed onset of extreme emotion, even though at the time of the event I don't think too much of it. For example, two weeks after going out with a friend, I started to experience severe shame only because she told me to put my phone away as there was a flash when I was taking a photo.

Feeling sporadic embarrassment is typical for humans, but my unconscious mind repeatedly scans for potential scenarios where I may have been treated unfairly. It especially enjoys seeking out daft events that may not have bothered me initially, and then brings it to the forefront of my conscious mind. That's when intense shame, anger, guilt or anxiety begins to flood in. Consequently, I get very strong urges to fight or destroy whatever triggered this. When, after days, the fixation eventually subsides, another immediately takes its place.

I reckon it stems from the helplessness I felt as a child when I couldn't defend myself. Now, when I've been compromised in some way, even in the slightest, I fixate and must battle extremely hard not to worsen things. Perhaps it's a reason why I struggle to maintain friends. I'm deeply observant of their behaviours, and should a person take a harmless "misstep," I withdraw and write them off.

I feel as if there is a judge recording every interaction I have. I'm in fear that something I say might bite me later. I am paranoid about ensuring I communicate as effectively as I can, despite knowing how futile it is, because communication occurs on the listener's terms.

I incessantly reread everything: emails, text messages. I re-listen to audio notes many times to ensure I've left no stone unturned. I compulsively rehearse conversations in my head over mundane matters such as which entry ticket to buy for a friend, or informing another that I will be popping out for a bit. I do it to ensure that I am being as thorough as I can be. Leaving no room for misinterpretation to prevent things from "going south." And in case they do, I at least have that reassurance that everything was clear as could be from my end, and I can be absolved of all responsibility.

Limerence. Till recently, I've constantly had an individual to fixate on. Initially, it was an effective coping mechanism that I discovered at a very young age. It helped me dissociate from trauma at home, as well as succeed at whatever it was that I was doing. Whether it be a teacher I wanted to impress, or a corner shop cashier with whom to transact, that individual was the only source of dopamine I had. This rapidly escalated into Sex and Love addiction (SLA), to such an intense degree that I could not think about anything else. It was no longer pleasurable, but parasitic.

Co-dependency and fawning seep through into my relationships, as I'm skilful at accommodating the needs of my romantic partner, but clueless in knowing what mine are. Boundaries are non-existent and I struggle to do something just for myself without getting a seal of approval from a partner. It's not surprising, given the enmeshed nature of my upbringing.

When I have a joyful experience like discovering a volcanic view in Lanzarote, my first reaction is to share it with those for whom I care. I wish I knew how to savour certain moments for myself and myself only. Until my loved ones have experienced what I have, I'm prevented from enjoying the moment to its fullest.

Emotional dysregulation is the crux of the issue when it comes to people suffering from an overactive and highly sensitive nervous system. I do feel happy at times, though most of my life has been infected with anhedonia. I'm very envious of people despite counting my blessings. David Benatar has said that "most people believe that they were either benefited or at least not harmed by being brought into existence." I wish I was in that majority.

Two things have helped me feel better: taking medication, and practising DBT skills. However, medication made me rather numb to my emotions, and thus I made a deliberate choice to go cold turkey. That way, I knew I was practising skills with full effect. Afterall, they did say to "increase the skills and reduce the pills" during sessions.

That said, it's draining constantly to exert so much mental energy to function "healthily." Willpower does run out sometimes. I truly believe there is no point to life. Though it helps to *create* meaning for survival. I'm tired of being alive and sick of how fragile I constantly feel. It's like I'm a glass vase balancing on a road divider of the M25. I want to be a block of cement.

I understand that all humans feel negative emotions. Nonetheless, I've learnt through therapy that there is a drastic difference in how intensely I feel emotions in comparison with the average person *sans* my diagnosis. Despite having the security of knowing that I can fall back to tablets, I do have curiosity in seeing if I can turn my life around without dependence on medication.

I want my default response to hardship to be either effective problem-solving methods or radically accepting reality. These are better than expending energy to resist the urge to search YouTube for "how to tie the hangman's knot." I am mindful of "nature vs nurture." I cannot say with utter confidence that had my childhood not been the way it was, I wouldn't be the way I am. I openly tell my parents I would rather not of been born.

5

Living with Diabetes

Solomon Benatar

THE BEGINNING

I WAS DIAGNOSED WITH Type-1 diabetes when I was fifteen years old while on holiday from boarding school at our home in a small mining village in Southern Rhodesia. My mother sent me to see the only doctor in the village as I was always hungry and insatiably thirsty, yet steadily losing weight. The doctor's surgery was a five-minute walk from our home, and he had known me since he brought me into the world in the small local hospital. He immediately diagnosed diabetes and sent me home to pack a bag and wait for him to take me, accompanied by my mother, to the hospital. All of this within two hours of my consulting him.

It was lonely being the only patient in the hospital, where I spent almost a week learning the daily insulin regime and routine urine testing, as well as becoming familiar with the dietary restrictions required to achieve stabilisation of my blood sugar. I seemingly accepted the diagnosis with equanimity, and began to learn to live with its demands, determined not to let it interfere with my life more than necessary. I have no clear recollection of other emotions at that time, except that I was inspired to choose a career in medicine. I also recall reading a book about diabetes by a Dr Lawrence. Finding this to be inadequate for patients, I had the urge to write a more patient-oriented text—but did not make headway beyond an early draft. At that time (1957), the longest survival time on insulin was thirty-six years (insulin having been discovered in 1921). I have lived with diabetes for sixty-nine years, and am still counting, while writing of my experiences in the 105th year since the discovery of insulin!

In the early years, while at boarding school and in university residence, I became accustomed to, and reluctantly accepted, small amounts of low calorie, low fat, and often low taste food. I was constantly tempted to sample tastier food—and then regretted it when I had succumbed. This desire continues, although with some most welcome mitigation since being married. My dear wife's motivation to create the tastiest dishes from the humblest of low-calorie vegetables and other healthy foods—daily for over sixty years—with good cheer, love, and imagination, have made my meals enjoyable and diabetic-friendly.

Living with diabetes is unquestionably onerous and has become much more so in later life. A strict diet, meals at regular times, constantly being hungry, eyeing foods one should not eat, and frequent blood sugar testing are the daily intrusive and self-control burdens that continue relentlessly "24/7" throughout life. Socialising over meals has generally not been easy, as many consider diabetes to be a disease that requires avoiding sugar, and hosts are often surprised when one takes only small portions of fatty foods and rich pastas, or puddings, even those made without added sugar. One copes with unexpected variations by downplaying the problem and juggling insulin doses before meals. This is often difficult under circumstances when the exact mealtime and menu are unknown. Top up doses of insulin are also used if required and one becomes accustomed to this. During my teen and early adult years I was also often faced with well-intentioned people telling me of cures for diabetes and urging me to try these.

PROGRESS AND ADVANCES IN CARE

As the pancreas still produces some insulin in the early years of diabetes, one daily injection sufficed. Urine testing for glucose about three times daily was also adequate. After a few years, as spontaneous insulin production diminished, I reluctantly accepted the need for two injections a day and the introduction of a longer acting insulin. This seemed a major setback, with which I recall having some difficulty reconciling. Today I have at least five injections per day (four short-acting and one long-acting)—and sometimes additional short-acting shots if required. Initially I used bovine insulins and then moved on to synthetic insulins in the early 1990s.

A few years after starting synthetic insulin I developed proliferative retinopathy. I read of some reports in the UK Independent Diabetes Trust Magazine that this had occurred in other patients who had switched and who had improved after returning to the original animal insulins. Although this was only anecdotal evidence, I reverted to animal insulins. These became increasingly difficult to obtain, but I managed to do so through friends in the UK during my frequent academic travels. It is not clear whether reversion to these was of any benefit to me, and some years later a diabetologist in Toronto strongly recommended that I use the synthetic insulins, which I have used without any problems.

The injection hygiene regimen has evolved slowly over the decades. In the early years, needles and breakable glass syringes were kept sterile in methylated spirits when not in use, and then immersed in freshly boiled water and allowed to cool before use. The transition from thick, long metal needles, used multiple times (because of expense) until they became blunt—often with a barb—before being discarded, through to modern disposable plastic pen-set syringes, with short and very thin needles, has been a most welcome advance. The ease and painlessness of these modern injections have made them the least unpleasant aspect of the disease. In the early years of my illness when it was not possible to measure one's own blood glucose, the major concerns were avoiding hypoglycemic attacks, which one could sense, and high blood sugar levels that were only revealed by the presence of glucose in the urine.

Another advance that eased daily life were the serial transitions from cumbersome testing of levels of glucose in urine, through invasive blood glucose testing (multiple finger-pricks daily) and ultimately to non-invasive testing of blood glucose. Initially, urine testing comprised boiling Benedict's solution in a test-tube heated over a methylated spirits burner after adding several drops of freshly passed urine. Then came Clinitest tablets that induced spontaneous boiling in a test tube, followed by Dipstix urine testing, and later the Glucometer for finger-prick blood sugar testing (five to six times each day). After finger-pricking for many decades it was difficult to produce good fingerprints on fingerprint registering— a recurrent, but admittedly minor irritation when entering the USA on many occasions.

The availability in recent years of the Freestyle Libre flash drive reader and interstitial glucose sensor has been a boon. In addition to the ease of testing dozens of times a day, the ability to record each activity of significance—when and what one eats, the time and dose of insulin, when one exercises—and to calculate appropriate insulin doses with estimated food intake, and detailed graphic records stored on a portable reader programme transferable to one's laptop, makes for much more effective and easy control within a narrower range of blood glucose levels. A diabetes nurse educator in Toronto in the 2010s was of great assistance in helping me become accustomed to the intricacy of achieving better control with this device, and I strongly recommend that all with diabetes take advantage of such assistance if available. The cost of the sensors is very high and surely far outstrips production costs. Similarly, the cost of finger prick precision strips seemed unreasonable. The medical device business, like the drug industry is geared towards excessive profits rather than to improving health. This is a sad reflection of how medicine has become commercialised and beyond the reach of many.

One of the difficulties when endogenous insulin is no longer produced, is that when the effect of each dose of short-acting insulin ends, even the smallest portion of food raises the blood sugar. This is most frustrating and leads to some obsession with very frequent non-invasive measurements (about twenty-five each day) and enhanced efforts to keep blood glucose within a narrow range. Anxiety, feelings of frailty, and of possible loss of consciousness associated with hypoglycemia, are accompaniments of rigidly tight control.

Symptoms of hypoglycemia include anxiety, rapid pulse rate, sweating, some disorientation, the urge to have something sweet or to eat otherwise unallowed foods—such as cake or chocolate. It is easy to overeat and then to face the rebound raised blood glucose and a "washed-out" feeling when the episode is over. Self-discipline is required to avoid hypoglycemia. It is necessary to be vigilant and to always have some form of "sweetmeat" easily available in the event of hypoglycemic attacks. Fortunately, I have never experienced hypo- or hyperglycaemic coma and I am appreciative of always sensing when my blood sugar is falling to "hypo" levels. The availability of HbA1c measurements that provide insight into overall control over three-month periods is of great value in achieving tighter control. However, between measurements there is inevitable associated anxiety that one might not be achieving the best possible control from hour to hour over every twenty-four-hour period. I have come to accept some "bad" days with less adequate control as par for the course!

COMPLICATIONS

During the early years, it was easier to lead an almost normal life, but this became more difficult with the restrictions associated with aging and the development of some of the myriad complications arising from long standing effects of diabetes that take their toll on the quality of life. As a physician, I have deeper insights into these than most patients. The advantage in understanding how to achieve good control and detect warning symptoms early is associated with the disadvantage of being so well-informed that anxiety about the future is increased.

My earliest complication was proliferative retinopathy with recurrent retinal bleeds resulting in recurrent episodes of temporary loss of vision, with slow recovery as the blood in the vitreous humour was absorbed. Repeated retinal laser surgeries over several years were stressful (and often quite painful with many hundreds of "shots" at each session). However, these successfully interrupted progress of the retinopathy. The many hours spent in waiting rooms prior to laser sessions tested one's patience during a busy working life, but I was always grateful to have had access to such treatments from skilled colleagues both in Cape Town and in Toronto. Ongoing fears from early warnings that I could probably be blind within ten years were depressing, especially as my work and leisure pursuits were dependent on reading and writing. The love and caring of my dear wife, who affirmed her constant availability to read to me should this become necessary, was most comforting. Gradual visual deterioration over fifteen years led to my failing the eye test when I tried to renew my driver's licence. Sequential bilateral phaco-vitrectomies (removal of the vitreous humour and lens, and replacement of the lens) were miraculous in restoring my vision, and later, my driver's licence.

It was very disappointing to discover after the first operation that the wrong lens had been inserted. Prior to the surgery I had opted for the choice of lenses that would allow me to read without spectacles, and to use spectacles only for long term vision, to which I had become accustomed over many years. However, the lenses inserted required spectacles for reading and not for long-range vision! It is not clear how this error arose as I had indicated my preference to the technician, when she did the IOL Master test (ocular biometry performed with the ZEISS IOLMaster device) and ordered the lenses. It has been somewhat disconcerting to have to tolerate this unselected outcome, that necessitates having reading glasses scattered through our apartment, but I am grateful for being able to see so well again.

Without endeavouring to find out how this error arose or to blame anyone, I adjusted with minimal angst.

Another complication, peripheral neuropathy (degeneration of the ends of long nerves), has manifest in progressive numbness of both feet and some loss of position sense, with resultant disturbance of gait and tendency to falls – aggravated by some loss of peripheral vision from repeated laser treatments. In addition to being uncomfortably aware of dysesthesia in my feet, I regularly check for foot injuries and infections, that because of impaired sensation could lead to amputations. I have maintained good foot hygiene and fortunately avoided these limb complications. In one of my falls, I injured my left foot and developed severe oedema for several months. Charcot's foot, another complication of the disease, was diagnosed, and I had to wear an air boot for a prolonged period. Recovery was so slow that I feared the possibility of never again being able to take my much-enjoyed daily walks. Within a year or so, I was able to do so, and by 2021 I was walking several kilometers each day which is therapeutic in many ways. Fortunately, I have not had neuropathic pain that afflicts some patients with diabetes. In my late seventies I took to walking with a stick to assist my balance and to avoid falling.

A serious complication of major ongoing concern was the development of coronary artery disease. This manifested with mild symptoms for the first time when I was recovering after surgery for a (right) shoulder replacement. Several weeks later, visualization of blood flow through the coronary arteries, achieved by injecting dye through a catheter passed from the radial artery at the wrist into the aorta, showed diffuse disease with severe stenosis of the left main coronary artery. Several stents were inserted. Angina a few months later led to strong recommendations for triple bypass surgery. Having suffered considerably from complications of the shoulder surgery, I was reluctant to have another surgical procedure with anticipated prolonged suffering, and I was concerned about renal failure due to exacerbation of any renal damage I may have had from long standing diabetes. Of even greater concern was the thought of possible cerebral damage during cardiac bypass.

My reluctance to have major surgery against the background of fifty-seven years of diabetes was overcome by expert, gracious, and patient explanations from my cardiologist and cardiac surgeon. Both had been outstanding trainees during my headship of our university and hospital department of medicine, and I had great confidence in them. They were optimistic that despite my long-standing diabetes, I would do well given my good state of general health, almost normal renal function for my age, good run-off coronary arteries on which to place the grafts, and well-preserved cardiac function. The statistically estimated operative mortality risk of about two- to three- percent was accepted, and I and my family all agreed with the decision to go ahead. Before surgery, I wrote a detailed advance care directive, with the assistance and agreement of my family, to ensure that I would not be kept alive should severe complications develop.

After completion of the surgery, I was kept in a controlled coma and on artificial ventilation for twenty-four hours. The post-operative ICU experience of vivid and deeply disturbing hallucinations for a few days, after regaining consciousness and being disconnected from the ventilator, was unequivocally the worst and most terrifying experience of my life. The hallucinations gradually subsided after about forty-eight hours, initially only when my eyes were open, but persisting when they were closed. I subsequently learned that the hallucinations were probably caused by the benzodiazepines used to keep me in a controlled coma—and their use has since been avoided when I have undergone other surgical procedures.

Gradual progression of coronary artery disease over the next seven years led to several more coronary artery interventions. These included insertion of multiple stents, their subsequent occlusion by inflammatory and atherosclerotic stenoses that were treated successfully with angioplasties using cutting, drug eluting balloons, (procedures used to unblock the stents), and follow-up coronary angiograms when new symptoms developed. These findings and procedures made me realize that my long-term prognosis was significantly compromised and encouraged me to rethink how I would lead my life over the coming years. I continued to lead as normal a life as possible, while remaining on multiple medications and maintaining strict control of my blood glucose and lipid levels. I also continued to take daily exercise in the hope of slowing the relentless progression of the coronary artery disease—but knowing that progression would be inevitable. I appreciate each and every day for being as well as I am, and for being able to do whatever I want to do—and in my own time.

Another complication from the many years of fragmented sleep following my severe shoulder injury was the onset of severe restless legs syndrome involving upper and lower limbs and requiring daily treatment with a dopamine agonist. Although this effectively suppresses the abnormal movements, I continue to have many hours awake at night. My mind is alert during these hours in which I enjoy reading and writing as well as listening to music. I accept the need for short power naps in the daytime—and enjoy these too.

SOME CONCLUDING THOUGHTS

Living with diabetes is a demanding and wearisome life-sentence with no parole. There is a need for adaptation with stoicism and avoidance of excessive introspection. In addition to being grateful for the very excellent treatment I have been privileged to receive from colleagues, many of whom trained under my guidance, I have enjoyed a most supportive family, comfortable living conditions and many other reasons to be grateful. The first is that despite a strong correlation between small-vessel ocular complications of long-standing diabetes with small vessel kidney disease and chronic renal failure, I have no signs of diabetic renal disease. The possibility of chronic renal dialysis has long haunted me, and I am infinitely grateful for having been spared this to date. The second reason is that I have been spared atherosclerosis of large vessels in my legs that could have led to the amputations so common in patients with diabetes. Last, but certainly not least, I have not developed any cerebrovascular disease.

Many of my friends and classmates who were physically stronger than I am, and who lived lives without chronic illnesses, have died before me. Reflecting on my life has made me realise that living with diabetes has enabled me to look after myself better than I might have done, and thus probably given me extra years of life. I have eaten healthily, exercised regularly, taken good care of my feet, refrained from smoking, and have only taken alcohol in moderation. But I have missed feeling as strong as I would like to be and therefore unable to be much more vigorously active physically.

Awareness of my own suffering and of the loneliness of suffering have sensitised me as a person and a physician, enabling me to connect and communicate more effectively with many of my patients and their families. Although no longer practising, I am frequently contacted for advice by friends and others and am always pleased to be able to provide what I hope are balanced perspectives on problems others are facing.

I have continued to read and to write academic articles, as well as taking daily walks with family and friends, although my enthusiasm and ability to do so have gradually diminished. As I have become older, I have, with regret, developed a "shorter fuse," and increasingly need more quiet time without extraneous sensory input other than beautiful music. Although I get weary more easily, I do not feel I am as old as I am in years, and I want to continue living for as long as I can be independent and intellectually stimulated. For those who live with diabetes, I conclude on this note of encouragement that with self-discipline and resilience, a productive, satisfying life is achievable. A new advance in treating diabetes with transplantation of gene-edited pancreatic cells offers a most exciting potential cure for diabetes.

6

Living with Disfigurement

Henrietta Rose-Innes

I'm writing this very far from home, in a hushed white landscape. I am at a writers' residency in New England, the only person who's travelled here from another continent. These days have been strange, portentous: unseasonal ice storms and deep snowfall, earthquakes in New York, wildfires at home in Cape Town. Last week, a total eclipse of the sun manifested in the sky directly above this little Maine town. I sat shivering on the edge of a frozen lake, upturned face stiff in the cold, as the moon progressed across the solar disc and everything held its breath.

I have been a fiction writer, and I've come here to see if I can be that again. A bad thing happened to me in 2021, and since then I just haven't found the words. Or rather, something bad had been happening to me for years before that, perhaps decades, but 2021 was when it surfaced—literally, a painful lump erupting from my gum and pushing out my molars.

The cancer that was revealed to be hiding in my jaw required significant surgery. Hallucinating on morphine in the ICU, I understood that my head had been replaced by the unendurably heavy metal head of a robot, and that the nurses and orderlies were demons plotting to kill me. I was unable to open my rebuilt mouth to speak, and so I wrote notes to the doctors in a little notebook with a neon-orange cover: paranoid and inscrutable instructions, complaints, and pleas for rescue.

In radiotherapy I was restrained by a thermoplastic shell, molded to my features, that gripped my face, neck and shoulders like a partial sarcophagus. During one session, as the heavy machine revolved around me spitting beams, I breathed in but somehow could not exhale, tongue pressing my lips against the mask. I lay there, quite calm, running out of air as the nurses scrambled from the observation room to extract me.

I know that I'm lucky. I had the best surgeons, medical aid, a successful outcome, and support at home. The scars on my throat and neck and lips and chin and inside my mouth cannot be considered terrible disfigurement on the scale of burns or bullet wounds, and they will not kill me, as the cancer would eventually have done. My head came out of treatment the size of a small microwave oven, but it has since subsided to human dimensions. A hundred years ago, a person with this condition would have had their jaw entirely removed. I'm ok.

But still, I'm left with this distortion, this skewness. Pain that comes and goes. Parts that feel alien or numb to my fingertips. I have some difficulties with eating, with speaking, with the damage done by radiation to teeth and bone and tissue. In a minor but humiliating flourish, I now cannot put even the mildest of spicy foods in my mouth without palpitations. Scar tissue and tides of oedema stiffen my jaw and throat, and sometimes my nightmares play out inside a heavy robot head.

Face masks were a blessing. During the pandemic I could pretend for a while that the change to my appearance was not real, because people could not see it. But they see it now. Each time I bump into an old acquaintance, I have to tell my story again. Friends I've known since school have looked me in the eye without recognition.

Strangers mostly treat me with unusual solicitousness, like an invalid or a very old person. They can be startlingly direct: "*What happened to you?*" One young supermarket cashier told me that my misfortune was what she most feared for her own future. I've had people burst into tears at the sight of me, discreetly pay for my order at a coffee shop where I sat reading, or tell me that I reminded them of dead or disabled relatives. A handful of times, I've been approached by evangelicals who invite me to church and tell me God loves me. It surprises me every time—I can forget that I'm seen. I don't really mind the forthrightness, but I miss invisibility.

Other days, with other people, I think it's really not so bad. From the nose up, it's still me. But the discomfort distances me. When I may seem to be listening to someone speak, I'm often secretly preoccupied, feeling with my tongue around the altered landscape of my mouth—patches of skin where there's no sensation, patches where there's too much. I cannot smile like I used to, showing my teeth.

All in all, I am muted. This is not the worst thing in the world: I'm partial to quiet. (Sometimes it's convenient to pretend that speaking is harder than it actually is.) But I miss easy joking, unselfconscious chat. These days people often tell me to speak up; my words are softer and more blurred than they sound in my own ears, and certain letters are difficult. My tongue can't roll an R, for example. I cover my mouth in conversation because I'm not altogether in control of how it moves or looks. Before, I gave talks and readings, but now I can't speak continuously for long before I feel something like a hard hand closing around my throat. I don't have to worry about all this when I'm alone, and so I am alone quite a lot.

About the cancer itself I am, perhaps oddly, incurious. It was rare and unlucky. In other ways lucky: it didn't spread to my lungs, the most likely route for this type of tumor. It is gone now, and at this point it seems probable that it won't return. There is nothing I could have done to avoid it, no better care I could have received; not much more I can do to fix what I have. I press on: see my doctors, apply creams, avoid mirrors. I apply for writer's residencies. I'm not yet brave enough to update my author's photo.

Last week, as the sun pulled clear, you could hear the whole town cheering across the ice as the brief strange nightfall reversed itself. A half-dozen resident artists and writers were gathered on deckchairs on the hill above me, eating popcorn, wearing tin-foil hats and cardboard spectacles with tinted lenses. They weren't watching me but I'm there in many of their photographs, a small figure down on the edge of the lake, too far away for my expression to be legible. I may have waved.

I'm not so good with non-fiction. I had to force myself to write this, slogging all through the night, snow beating at the windowpanes, the sun on the far side of the world. This is not what I planned to do when I came here.

But something had made me pack that desperate orange notebook. I hadn't looked at it since the hospital. Yesterday, as I searched for a way to approach the topic of my condition, I steeled myself to read my own dimly remembered, urgent missives from intensive care.

It was impossible. My handwriting was incomprehensible, a woozy scrawl trailing off the page. The notes were meaningless. I closed the orange book and put it away.

I am trying to speak more clearly now.

7

Living with Depression

Anton Fagan

There were warning signs, to be sure. But they became apparent only with hindsight. When the depression struck, I was not expecting it. And, not expecting it, I was wholly unprepared for the havoc it would wreak in my life and the lives of others.

I had some familiarity with depression, but only as a condition suffered by others. When I was sixteen, I saw my older brother Eduard curled in a foetal position on his bed, day after day, with my mother sitting close, listening and talking with inexhaustible patience. Six years later my younger brother Francois took his own life. He was an introvert. So, none of us had known that he was depressed, even though he, Eduard, and I were living at home at the time. Eduard had often spoken of suicide during his depression. But for him it had been an abstract idea, to be endlessly turned over in thought and conversation. For Francois, suicide was a concrete action, to be executed properly, just that once, in the family garage, only hours after we had together watched a comedy on TV.

Nor, therefore, was I unfamiliar with grief. I had shared a bedroom with Francois for sixteen years, from the age of two to the age of eighteen. For eight of those years, he and I had walked to school together, every weekday throughout the school term. When little, we had built tree houses and spent nights camping in the garden. As teenagers, we had slept on Devil's

Peak and windsurfed on the Breede River. Losing Francois, when he was twenty and I was twenty-two, was like having a limb severed. The pain of it was so intense that at times I felt that I was going insane. But Francois's death did not cause me to sink into depression – at least not in a form which I recognised as such.

Anxiety was not something I had previously encountered. Yes, of course, I had both experienced and observed the ordinary "butterflies-in-the-stomach" kind of anxiety that is commonplace before writing an examination, taking a driver's test, or giving a wedding speech. Indeed, for twenty-five years I had sought out this kind of anxiety, every weekend, when climbing on Table Mountain or Lion's Head. As if that were not enough, I had also, after a break of more than fifteen years, taken up windsurfing again, on a short board in thirty-knot southeasterly winds, constantly on the verge of losing control. And I had bought a motorbike, so that I could once again arrive at work exhilarated, rather than wearied, by my daily commute.

But that is not the kind of anxiety I am talking about here. I am talking about the kind of anxiety that renders you incapable of doing your job, driving your car, or even walking out of the front door of your house. It is the kind of anxiety that has you pacing through your home, day in and day out, unable to lie down, sit still, or even stand in one place for more than a few moments. It is the kind of anxiety that gives you restless legs and pins and needles in your hands and arms, and so fatigues you that by eight in the evening you can hardly keep your eyes open, except that you know that, notwithstanding a double dose of sleeping pills, it will wake you up four hours after going to bed, and keep you tossing and turning for the rest of the night.

It was February 2022. COVID-19 having taken its toll on the nation, psychologists and psychiatrists were in short supply. But I was desperate. I had returned to work a month earlier, after a four-week vacation at the mouth of the Breede River, staying in the cottage which my parents had bought more than fifty years before, and in which I had spent every summer holiday since I was six. The first two weeks back passed uneventfully. But then my wife, Suzie, and I had an argument. She wanted me to do a "day skipper" course, so that, to celebrate her sixtieth birthday, we could take our children sailing in the Mediterranean. I resisted, on the ground that, given the time already taken up by my work and my climbing, I was "only just coping," and could not take on the additional burden.

It was a trivial dispute. Yet it tipped me over the brink. Though neither Suzie nor I knew this, I had been teetering at the edge of the precipice for months, and a tiny nudge was all it took to send me tumbling into the abyss. Two weeks later I was on a Selective Serotonin Reuptake Inhibitor (SSRI) called Cilift, anti-anxiety medication called Stresam, and sleeping pills called Z-Dorm—prescribed by my GP, as I had not yet managed to track down a psychiatrist who could fit me in for a consultation. I was also booked off on sick leave for the first time in a quarter of a century. However, though having time to kill, I was unable to go for a walk on the mountain or a swim at the beach. I was unable to read a book, watch a movie, or listen to music. I was incapable, even, of having an ordinary conversation.

I was afflicted by a kind of turbocharged anxiety. Some of my anxiety concerned the world around me, which had suddenly taken on a sinister and threatening character. I worried that my car might break down on the way to work, on the way to the climbing gym, on the way to the supermarket, or on the way to my son's school. I fretted that I did not know how to call an Uber, had never sent a WhatsApp message, and was yet to do my first EFT. I feared being mugged on Lion's Head or Table Mountain, or while walking from my home to the pharmacy three blocks away. It was this kind of anxiety, anxiety about the world, that would keep me under virtual house arrest in the months lying ahead.

However, my anxiety about the world was overlaid by anxiety of a second kind. It had, as its object, anxiety itself. It was anxiety about anxiety or, more accurately perhaps, about the possibility of becoming anxious. This second kind of anxiety—which, I would later learn, is called "anticipatory anxiety"—was no less debilitating than the first. It was the reason I could not read, watch movies, or have ordinary conversations. Lest something said made me anxious, I absented myself from family meals. And, when Suzie or the children had friends around, I hid in the bedroom. Suzie trawled our bookshelves for suitable novels: Jane Austen's *Persuasion*, Nick Hornby's *Juliet, Naked*, Dodie Smith's *I Capture the Castle*. But sooner or later, I would come across a passage that I feared would make me fearful, and that would be that.

"My brain: it's my second-favourite organ," says Woody Allen's character, Miles Monroe, in the movie *Sleeper*. In my case, the ordering of organs had always been reversed. I am an academic. Thinking is what I do for a living. That is true of many people. But it is, I believe, safe to say that I had prioritised thinking over feeling, or reason over emotion, more than most people do—not only in my professional, but also in my personal, life. That is most likely one of the reasons that climbing so appealed to me. It requires a constant subordination of emotion to reason: "I am frightened that I am going to fall and die" having to yield to "I know that the chances of me falling are negligible and that, even if I do, I am on a rope and the chances of it snapping are miniscule."

Within a fortnight of Suzie's and my tiff, this ordering had been turned upside down. Every time that I felt anxiety about this or that trifling matter starting to well up inside of me, I would rehearse all the reasons that I really had no cause for concern. But it was useless. I could no longer rely on reason to keep my emotions (in this case wayward ones) in check. I was no longer able, by an act of thinking, to force my feelings into a submission. It was not so much that my emotions now dominated my reasoning. It was rather that my emotions had been completely untethered, or cut loose, from my reasoning. They lived in my body. But, rather like alien invaders, they led their lives according to their own design.

Accompanying my anxiety was a hypersensitivity to sound. Cape Town is a big, bustling city. At night you can hear dogs barking, alarms blaring, and sirens wailing. But only if you make a conscious effort to listen out for them. Having lived most of my life in the city, I had become oblivious to these noises. But now the distant barking of a dog or wailing of a siren would slice through my filters, instantly putting me into a state of apprehensive alertness. My sensitivity to sound went beyond this. When members of my family spoke to me, it sometimes felt as though my ears were being buffeted by their words, not metaphorically, but literally. However, it was worse when they fell silent, and the house grew quiet. Then I would hear the inner workings of my own body: a persistent hissing noise in my ears. This was not that different from hearing voices in my head—a sure sign of madness.

For the first time in my life, I tried meditation. However, whenever I attempted one of the prescribed breathing routines in the stillness of my bedroom, I would become fixated on the sounds in my head. In desperation, I started meditating with an app called *The Daily Calm*. The background noise of rustling leaves, falling rain, or a crackling fire, as well as Tamara Levitt's dulcet tones, served to drown out the hissing in my ears. But even *The Daily Calm* occasionally misfired, as when Ms Levitt, in her soothing, reassuring voice, shared the not-so-soothing-and-reassuring fact that, when he was already an influential psychiatrist, Carl Jung suffered a mental health crisis, with "intense emotions, dreams, and even terrifying visions," which necessitated his withdrawal "from his professional work for several years."

In March, I finally managed to get an appointment with a psychiatrist. I had to rely on Suzie to get me there, even though it was only a ten-minute drive away. At our first meeting, the psychiatrist mentioned the D-word. So had my psychologist, a few weeks previously. I had immediately dismissed it. In my view, it did not fit my symptoms. After all, I was stressed, fearful, and anxious, not sad or miserable. More than that, I was not that guy. And I most certainly did not want to be him. On the one hand, in a country with widespread poverty, I led a life that would be the envy of ninety-nine per cent of the world's population. How could I be depressed? How dared I be? On the other hand, I was still labouring under the delusion—or at any rate clinging to the hope—that, as rapid as had been my descent into madness, so would be my ascent back to normality. But depression, I knew, or feared, was a long-term thing.

After I had been on Cilift for two months, with no improvement in my condition, my psychiatrist put me onto a second SSRI, called Serdep. This likewise produced no change. I started to worry that I might never recover. It was clear to me that, unless my condition improved, my life would not be worth living. Less clear to me was how I would end it. I had accumulated a largish stash of Z-Dorm and Stresam. But the prospect of a botched job that left me alive but brain damaged was not appealing. A more attractive option, by far, was to hurl myself off the top of Table Mountain. But it seemed an awful imposition on the members of Mountain Rescue, upon whom would fall the unpleasant task of removing my mangled corpse. And it was not easily squared with my strong aversion to mountain litter (and litterers). In any event, I had not yet relinquished all hope of recovery: so, for me, as for my brother Eduard many years before, suicide remained a theoretical notion.

Two SSRIs having failed, my psychiatrist decided to try something different, namely a Serotonin and Noradrenaline Reuptake Inhibitor (SNRI) called Venlor. It turned out to be a case of third time lucky. After a couple of weeks, my anxiety started to abate. But I was not yet out of the woods. My psychiatrist had diagnosed me as being in the midst of a "major depressive episode." The anxiety I was feeling, she had explained, was merely a byproduct, or manifestation, of that. Moreover, my anxiety was serving to mask my depression. However, once my anxiety began to recede, the depression which was its underlying cause would gradually reveal itself. I very much wanted my psychiatrist to be mistaken. But she was not. I had been, and still was, depressed. And, as my anxiety retreated, this became increasingly apparent.

Suzie's and my bedroom has a north-facing sash window. Pushed against its sill is a couch. When the weather is good (which it mostly is in Cape Town), the couch is sun-drenched from around eight in the morning until about one in the afternoon. I had been unable to sit on it (or anything else) while my anxiety had been acute. But now that my anxiety had lessened, I was again able to do so. And do so I did, pretty much all day, every day—with my eyes closed most of the time. Notwithstanding my depressed state, it did, I think, give me some pleasure to sit there, basking in the sunlight: I certainly missed the warmth and brightness whenever the sun disappeared behind a cloud. But that was not my reason for sitting there. My reason for sitting there was that I was unable to motivate myself to do anything else.

As Suzie went off in the morning, to take our younger son to school, she would say: "I want you to be showered by the time I get back." But when she returned two hours later, having done the drop off, walked on Camps Bay beach, and swum in the icy Atlantic, she would find me still slumped on the couch. The problem was not a lack of desire on my part. I wanted to get into the shower. I formed the will or intention to do so. But I was incapable of executing my will or carrying out my intention. I would sit there for hours, exhorting myself to "Go and have a shower. Go and have a shower. Go and have a shower." Many times, this would carry on well into the afternoon. And, when I eventually did overcome my inertia, and had gotten myself washed and dressed, I would usually go straight back to my seat on the couch—much to Suzie's consternation.

It is not that I did nothing, while sitting there, for weeks on end, with my eyes shut. I did a lot of thinking. Some of it concerned the actions I was too lethargic to perform. But mostly it was about my past, and it generally concerned my inadequacies, failures, and transgressions. I agonized about the fact that I had not obtained a first for my BA at Oxford, a failure which had left me with an ineradicable sense of intellectual mediocrity, even though I had subsequently gone on to complete a DPhil there. I thought, with shame, about the four-day affair I had had with a cousin, when I was twenty and she eighteen, thereby breaking one of the taboos that kept my extended family cemented together. And I reflected, with regret, upon the skills and abilities which, though they had taken time and effort to acquire, I was, through long neglect, busy losing (such as playing the guitar and reading Latin).

My mother-in-law, when comforting someone who was facing adversity or dealing with misfortune, was wont to use the adage: "And this too shall pass." I do not know whether it was due only to the Venlor, or also to the twice-weekly sessions I was having with my psychologist. Nor do I know how great a role was played by the simple passage of time. But maybe one month, maybe two, after my anxiety had started abating, I noticed that my depression had begun to do so too. The first activity I managed to engage in was to study German. This is not as odd as it may seem. For one thing, I could do it without moving off the couch. For another, my German grammar and vocabulary books, unlike the novels I had abandoned, were unlikely to ambush me with an anxiety-inducing or emotionally-taxing passage. Furthermore, by refreshing my German, I was holding the decline of at least one of my abilities in check.

Slowly but surely, my range of activities expanded (and my time on the couch correspondingly contracted). I started walking on the mountain and the beach again, and having the occasional plunge in the ocean. For months, the only music I had been able to listen to was Bach's Brandenburg Concertos (and, even then, only a particular recording thereof). Now I was once more able to enjoy John Lee Hooker, Bob Dylan, and Amy Winehouse. I wrote and completed two articles on the South African law of defamation—which was just as well, as my sick leave had expired, to be replaced by a six-month sabbatical. And I gradually recovered my libido, which, notwithstanding my disagreement with Mr Monroe (and perhaps also Mr Allen) about the proper rank-ordering of bodily organs, came as a relief to me.

In February 2023—exactly one year after my original collapse—I was lecturing again: or, at least, I would have been if my university had not been "shut down" for a week by protesting students. I had resumed my climbing three months before that. And, around Christmas and New Year, I had managed to get some windsurfing in at the mouth of the Breede River. But I was still in therapy. And, though I had weaned myself off Z-Dorm and Stresam, I was still on Venlor. Moreover, though I no longer passed my days sitting on the couch, and generally got myself showered immediately after deciding to do so, I had not recovered my former drive and spent an hour or more, almost every day, collapsed in a chair with my eyes closed. I also had not recovered my ability to read novels and general non-fiction, though I was able to read whatever was necessary for my teaching and writing. As for movies and series, I could not watch anything violent or harrowing, but coped fine with *University Challenge* and *Ted Lasso*.

The improvement in my condition had not been accomplished alone. Nor could it have been. Apart from the professional help I received, I also received invaluable support from family and friends. For an entire year, my brother Eduard phoned me every day—notwithstanding the fact that he is a senior counsel with a busy practice that consumes too much of his time. For about four months, when my anxiety and depression were at their worst, I phoned my ninety-one-year-old mother daily, ostensibly to report on my condition, but really just to hear her voice. During that same period, one old friend popped in once a week, to see how I was getting along. Another came around once a fortnight. These visits must have been an endurance for them. They were under strict orders not to mention anything that might make me anxious. That ruled out so many topics that every conversation quickly morphed into a self-centred—and no doubt tedious— monologue about me and my mental health.

Towering above the rest was my wife, Suzie. Suzie tends to be impatient with my maladies—understandably, as my obsession with climbing inclines me to treat every sniffle as a calamity. And she did a few times leave me feeling abandoned, such as when, only weeks after my initial collapse, she went off on a five-day hike with friends. But the hike had been a year in the planning and one of her friends had flown in from New York for it. More than that, Suzie had to remain strong, not only for my sake, but also for hers, and for that of our children, the youngest of whom still lives at home, the older two of whom happened to be at home when my anxiety and depression were at their worst. It was therefore crucial that Suzie not be sucked into my bleak and despairing world. Moreover, some of my biggest breakthroughs occurred when she was gone: I started driving again because she was not there to do the school run; I ventured out to the shops again because she was not there to buy the groceries.

My psychiatrist had impressed upon me the importance of "positive feedback loops." What she meant by this is that, even if going for a walk (or a swim, or lunch with a colleague) was the last thing I felt like doing, I should force myself to do it, because it would lift my mood just a tiny bit, so that, next time, it would be just that little bit easier to go for a walk, which would lift my mood just a tiny bit more, and so on. However, when you are depressed, it is hard to set this virtuous circle in motion. It helps if there is someone else who can cajole you, even goad you, into action. Suzie did this admirably. It is no exaggeration to say that, without her persistent (and insistent) prodding, I might still be languishing on the couch.

As I write these words, it is eighteen months since I first fell apart. In the past six months I have driven a four-by-four across Botswana with my family and friends. I have bungee jumped with two of my children and gone skydiving with the third. I have been climbing every week. I have survived three terms of lecturing, notwithstanding the fact that one of my lectures was invaded by protesting students and that their sympathisers tried (unsuccessfully) to have me "disciplined" for lampooning the protests in correspondence with one of my classes. I have even begun to give serious consideration to the possibility of doing a day skipper course. Does this mean that I am no longer "living with depression", so that my story really does not belong in this book?

I wish it did. However, I am still on Venlor, in an unreduced dose. I still see my psychologist twice every week. I am still unable to read for pleasure. I still cannot watch *The Wire*. And I still spend up to an hour every day just sitting, eyes closed, thinking unproductive thoughts. True, I did manage to clamber my way out of the chasm into which I had tumbled, and to step away from its edge. But it remains uncomfortably close. Suzie, who knows me better than anyone else does, is convinced that what I experienced last year was a once-off, brought about by a perfect storm of unhappy events: several years of student protests at my university; COVID-19 and the remote teaching it required; the departure of a small child whom we had fostered (and loved) for two years; and a family rift (since mended) for which I was partly responsible. I very much hope that Suzie is right. But the possibility that she might not be is a constant worry.

8

Living with an Eating Disorder

Anna Reyksík

Lying in bed at night, I often flip through old photos on my phone, hoping that the familiar images will help to soothe my tightly coiled body and restless mind. The most comforting pictures are those of my dad bopping around our living room with Meowstro — our grumpy-looking cat — in his arms, or photobombing the otherwise serious but lovely shots of one of my sisters and her then-new fiancé. I can't help but smile when I revisit the moments captured by those pictures. The mischief and the joyful lightness are palpable. But then, inevitably, I come upon a photograph of myself from just before what I now refer to as "the crash of 2018." These images rouse something more complicated in me.

On the one hand, they bring back memories of near-constant exhaustion and an inability to engage meaningfully with anything or anyone in the world. "Tired to the core" is how I felt for the ten or so years leading up to that crash. A part of me *really* can see that the body in which I was dragging myself around was not healthy. Isn't it ironic how the body can be both so light and yet also feel so weighed down by the burden of being? Nonetheless, I look at that body with a great longing. In that body, I did not feel quite so grotesque. Under my bed covers, I pinch some of the flesh around my waist . . . my "curve creators." Yuck.

I ache to shed it all—this flesh, this weight, this softness that feels so foreign. I cannot quite believe that I allowed myself to regain it. I feel as though I dropped my guard for just a moment and that the next thing I knew, I was rounded and unrecognizable . . . monstrous. I feel this most acutely when I press old clothes against this new body. My old pants would certainly have these new thighs in a chokehold. These new thighs—now touching each other—look and feel too much to bear. Fistful after fistful of dimply matter wrapped around my leg bones. Unwelcome. Revolting. And when I run, I feel all of those layers lurching, jiggling, and echoing with every thunderous step. All of that movement is obscene.

Despite the intense discomfort I feel inhabiting this new corpulent covering, I know all too well what it will take from me to be free of it. Initially, I will have to ignore my body's increasingly desperate pleas for nutrition. Of course, some requests will slip through. But I will have to take the utmost care to feed it only high-fibre vegetables and some protein. I will also drink water. So much water. Carbonated water, ideally, to drown out the incessant nagging for sustenance.

It is still amazing to me how quickly a body can adjust to this kind of deprivation. That said, just when you think that you have tamed the beast, the self-denial and flood of fluids will begin to erode your defences. Sticking to your plan will suddenly require that you find within yourself a commitment to asceticism that you could not previously have imagined. And if you do find such commitment, acting upon it will begin to strip you bare. It will take from you not just flesh, but your clarity of thought, sense of humour, interests, and patience with, and care for, others. It will snatch your sparkle, and soon you'll find yourself hollowed out, a shell moving through a life that no longer feels like your own.

Shells do not weigh very much, however. And as you stand before the cold court of your bathroom mirror and step onto the scale, you will see the needle shifting in the right direction and you will experience an exhilaration like none you've ever felt before. The shedding of pound after suffocating pound will bring you *immense* satisfaction and pleasure. After all, when you are just a shell, you will live in an emaciated world, a world in which nothing is as good as skinny feels. Accordingly, just like any addict, you will become singularly focused. In this case, though, your fixation will be on proteins, fats, and carbohydrates. Each one measured, scrutinized, dreaded. You will become fluent in deception, an expert in denial, just so that your pants cling less tightly to your thighs, and your elasticated underpants leave no trace around your waist.

I can appreciate how ludicrous all of this sounds. As a soon-to-be middle-aged woman, I am mortified that I continue to be intent on being small enough to fit into a certain pair of pants. I now know what I stand to lose if I return to tethering my self-worth to the pursuit and achievement of this goal. It is also very difficult for me to fathom why—with everything else going on in my life and in the world around me—the desire to be agonizingly thin occupies so much of my head space.

My best guess is that there is no reasoning with shame. And the shame that I feel walking around in this body is excruciating. Even my earliest memories are soaked in shame about my body. When I was very little, many family holidays were spent with my cousins. I *adored* my cousins, all of whom were younger than me, and I looked forward to holidays with them. But unlike my cousins and my sisters, I was not a skinny child. I was not fat. But I certainly was not skinny. And my awareness of this intruded into almost every moment of our time together.

In the mornings, for example, everyone else would get dressed in one room. They would go through each other's suitcases, even swapping clothes with one another if both parties agreed. I ached to be a part of those happy exchanges. But as soon as they were sufficiently engrossed in their bartering, I would slink out of the room and into a private space to undress and attempt to conceal my body under oversized t-shirts and baggy shorts.

On most days, my shapeless clothing swallowed up just enough of my body-hatred to allow me to enjoy playing with my sisters and cousins. But when it came time to get clean, that hatred surged back. While my sisters and cousins stepped into our shared bath with an enviable lack of self-consciousness, I would dawdle, insisting on an ample layer of bath bubbles before slipping in to join them.

Swimming presented many challenges too. This was unfortunate because I loved to swim and was actually a very capable swimmer. But I don't think I will ever be able to forget the burning shame that consumed me when my best friend's little sister saw me in a swimming costume for the first time and, with innocent astonishment, marvelled aloud at the size of my thighs.

Neither will I ever be able to forget the hot humiliation of my gran slapping my hand away as I reached for an additional scoop of ice cream one Thanksgiving.

So, from a very early age, I hated my body and was determined to change it. It took time to figure out *how* to do this, however. But by the time I was twelve, I had learned that if I rarely confessed to being hungry, threw away my school lunch, and signed up for as many school sports as I could, my body would start to shrink to a more palatable size.

From that point onwards, my relationship with food became increasingly unhealthy. On some days I would eat nothing. I would go to bed feeling nauseated and jittery, but determined not to ruin what had been a "perfect" day. This idea of perfection, while useful at times, tripped me up more often than not.

A perfect day was one on which I did not deviate from my plan, which might have entailed eating only a certain number of calories, one particular food item, or nothing at all. The plans I made were almost always too ambitious. But my standards were so unforgiving that anything less than complete success felt like total failure. Even one carrot on a day on which the plan was to eat nothing constituted disaster.

That one unplanned carrot would have such a destabilizing effect on me that you would have thought I had eaten an *entire carrot cake . . . with extra frosting*! In my diseased mind, everything had essentially gone to hell. That being the case, any and every food item would suddenly become fair game. A starving maniac would burst from within me and, lacking all self-control, I might feverishly consume an entire fat-filled bag of peanuts, a packet of biscuits, as well as a large tub of ice cream.

Shortly thereafter, the weight of what I had done would take hold of me, dragging me into a crater of despair and self-loathing. In that unforgiving pit, I would feel all of the food I had just scarfed down breaking down, particle by particle. I would then feel these particles seeping through my stomach lining and into my thighs and butt, which, in my mind, would then begin to swell. Next, the clothing I was wearing would feel as though it was growing tight and panic would rise in me accordingly. The only thing left to do, it would seem, was to purge what remained in my stomach. And so, I would heave myself to the bathroom, press a trembling finger down my throat, and empty myself until my eyes were swollen and sore. "That will teach you, you despicable, weak-willed glutton."

Although it was not for lack of trying, it was not until I was well into my thirties that I succeeded in shrinking my body so much that my appearance shocked and concerned others. I remember arriving at my parents' home for the Christmas holidays and, after settling on the couch with a cup of tea, being asked, "Can we talk to you about something?" I'm not sure what I was expecting them to want to talk about, but it was most certainly not my body. I listened with astonishment as they told me that an acquaintance of mine had called them to register her deep concern about how unhealthy she felt I looked. I felt a prickle of rage upon hearing this news. How dare she?! I quickly prepared myself for an argument but was almost immediately overwhelmed by the heaviness of it all. Instead of rising up to defend my appearance and dietary regime, I found myself crumbling, acknowledging that I no longer had a clear sense of the difference between healthy and unhealthy, that I needed some help.

The intensity of that brief conversation knocked me to the floor, so to speak. Though I did not truly wish to change my body—or to relinquish any control over what I allowed into it—I simply did not have the strength to stand back up. And so, with reluctance, I agreed to take the first steps toward healing my relationship with food and its impact on my body.

It has now been seven years since the crash of 2018. How did the healing go, you may ask? Am I all better? In many ways, I have recovered from my eating disorder. I am less obsessive. I have gained weight. My body is no longer a source of shock and concern for others; it is unremarkable once again. But my internal dialogue remains relentless, tormenting. Much of the time, I am able to function alongside it, and sometimes I manage to soften it. But there is no doubt that a part of me is still desperate for a body that I know would be the death of all that is "me".

So, for me, this is what recovery looks like. It's not a clear severing of ties with a wholly unreasonable master. Rather, it is a daily negotiation. But I'm one hell of a negotiator now that my eyes are open to all that is at stake.

9

Living with Hemophilia

Jan Glazewski

INTRODUCTION

1985 was an eventful year. I was a young man of thirty-two, about to start my dream job at the University of Cape Town and contemplating marriage. But these hopes were dashed. I was diagnosed HIV positive - as a result of receiving contaminated blood products.

My medical problems started much earlier, at birth in 1953, when I was diagnosed with hemophilia—a blood clotting deficiency, the effects of which would cascade through my entire life, both physically and emotionally.

My eldest brother, whom I never met, was born more than a decade earlier in Romania but died in Palestine of internal bleeding at the age of three, from the same disease. My parents had fled Poland at the onset of World War II, made their way to Romania and ended up in the Middle East, where my father joined the allied forces. They were never to return to their homeland. Ultimately, they arrived by ship in South Africa in 1947 with three daughters—to make a new life and all that it entailed.

I was just a few days old and still in the maternity ward at a Paarl hospital in the Western Cape, when the doctor who delivered me insisted that I be circumcised.

"No, please no!" pleaded my gaunt father in his thick Polish accent. "He will bleed! He has just been diagnosed as a hemophiliac. His brother died as baby of internal bleeding," insisted my father.

"Vitamin K will do the trick," announced the doctor confidently. "A new treatment for this bleeding disorder. It will stop any bleeding. We must go ahead and circumcise him."

But Vitamin K is not used to treat hemophilia: it is used to treat a related bleeding disorder. As a result, I bled profusely. Incisions were made in my six-day-old ankles, with plastic tubes inserted into the veins so that I could receive life-saving blood. Over seventy years later, I still bear the scars. However, although I bled and bled, I wanted to live, refusing to go the way of my brother.

So began my lifelong challenges with hemophilia.

HEMOPHILIA: SOME BACKGROUND

Hemophilia is a genetic disorder, which causes a lack of blood clotting factor, resulting in both external and internal bleeding. It is a rare hereditary disease which affects mostly males, while women are carriers of the disease.

In my case my mother was a carrier, and none of her three daughters (my elder sisters) were affected. However, one of my sisters is a carrier and one of her grandsons is affected. John was born some six decades after me and had a close call days after his birth, because of severe internal bleeding in his torso. But, thanks to having been diagnosed at birth and having access to new and effective treatment, he survived and is now leading a semi-normal teenage life.

Hemophilia has been dubbed the "royal disease" as it was prevalent among the aristocratic families of Europe during the late eighteenth and early nineteenth centuries. Queen Victoria was a carrier, and not only was her son, Leopold, affected, but two of her daughters and her granddaughter, Alexandra, were carriers of the disease. As is well known, Alexandra became the Tsarina of Russia, having married Nicholas II. Their son Alexei, a hemophiliac who was treated by the notorious Rasputin, was next in line to the Tsar's throne, but the entire family was assassinated by the Bolsheviks in 1910. Whenever my condition crops up at dinner parties, I quip that my great-grandmother was a chambermaid in the Tsar's palace, although in practice this could not have been the cause, since the Tsarina was the carrier.

The term "hemophilia" refers to two groups that display an excessive bleeding disorder. Most commonly the term refers to Hemophilia A (HA), or classic hemophilia, (Factor VIII deficiency) which is the blood clotting factor that I lack. The second is Hemophilia B (HB), also dubbed 'Christmas disease' as it was first diagnosed in a patient named Stephan Christmas. Both the causative genes are situated on the X chromosome, and it is predominantly males that express the disease, but some females may also have a bleeding tendency although typically milder unless there are unusual circumstances. Birth incidence for HA is said to be one in 5000 males, but HB is less common.

There are gradations of the disease—mild, moderate, and severe—depending on how much Factor VIII (the blood clotting factor), the liver produces. In my case, it is zero. Being a severe hemophiliac, I bruise easily and bleed profusely if I cut myself. During the usual childhood process of losing my teeth, I bled extensively, leaving pillowcases covered in blood, much to the distress of my mother, who was seriously ill at the time.

My mother died of cervical cancer when I was seven and my father married a widow with eight children fairly soon afterwards. So apart from inheriting a blood disorder, I gained eight stepsiblings and later a half-brother and half-sister from the new marriage. That made 14 children in total, which ensured that I did not get too much parental attention, but having three elder sisters made up for that!

LIVING WITH THE CONSEQUENCES

One of my earliest memories is of standing on the stoep at our home near Durbanville. I had dropped a glass bottle and cut my big toe. Blood was flowing everywhere. I cannot remember much more than that I was rushed to Groote Schuur Hospital, a major undertaking for my parents in those days, as the farm my father was renting, was some distance from Cape Town. This was the first of many spells that I spent in hospital, from childhood to my teenage years.

I recollect sitting with my father as an outpatient on the hard hospital benches, waiting for my turn to be referred to the hematology clinic. In hindsight, this endless waiting was not necessary, as there was a dedicated hemophilia clinic at Red Cross Children's Hospital but my father, as a recently arrived immigrant, was not aware of that.

Living with Adversity

When I was eight or nine years old, I tried to learn to ride a bicycle at the neighbours, who lived across the field from us. I remember struggling to seat myself on the bike, putting my right foot on the ground, hoisting myself up, and pushing the pedal with my left foot. I slipped incessantly, hitting my groin on the crossbar. Clearly the bike was too big for me. But I eventually got it right, riding triumphantly in a full circle around their lawn without falling.

The next morning, I awoke with my groin feeling uncomfortable. I gingerly lifted the sheet and saw that my scrotum was purple and blue, and as large as a tennis ball. I alerted my two stepbrothers, with whom I shared an upstairs bedroom. My stepmother arrived, lifted the sheet, took one look, and dropped it immediately. "Oh, my goodness! We have to take you to hospital." So, once again, off to Groote Schuur I went.

A later memory is of a visit to the local dentist in Durbanville village, when his injection hit a vein and my entire jaw and cheekbone swelled. My father signed the consent paper for me to undergo a tracheotomy, as my breathing was compromised, but fortunately the swelling subsided after the first transfusion. I was told afterwards that a mass was said at our local Catholic church, praying for my recovery. This clearly did the trick.

I recollect sitting as a teenager in a windy corridor on a hospital bench, waiting for a porter to transfer me to the X-ray department. I was admonished by a passing doctor for reading my hospital folder. Puzzled, I asked myself, "Whose body is this anyway?"

Today, the most difficult aspect to cope with is the cumulative effect of internal bleeding into my joints—particularly into the so-called hinge joints—my ankles, knees and elbows. This damage results from everyday physical activities, such as kicking a ball as a child or walking down a mountain track.

As a result, since turning forty, I have had both knees replaced, my left ankle fused, and my right ankle replaced after my retirement. Later, despite COVID-19, I have had my left elbow replaced. It had been severely damaged over the years by digging in the garden, carrying heavy bags, hitting golf balls and other activities. Not only am I a problem case when going through airport security, but with so many joint replacements, it has occurred to me that eventually, I may have to have my head replaced as well!

Jan Glazewski—Living with Hemophilia

TREATMENT THROUGH THE YEARS

During my childhood I was treated with whole blood. But when I was about seven, it was discovered that the essential clotting factor is contained in the plasma (white cell) component, making the red cells superfluous in transfusions for hemophiliacs. The factor is administered intravenously, and this meant that, for the same volume received, I could get considerably more of the vital clotting agent. Depending on the severity of the internal bleed, I would be admitted to hospital for a week or two and treated with 500 ml of fresh plasma twice daily for a few days. The transfusion took up to 20 minutes from a drip next to my bed. Some doctors struggled more than others to find a suitable vein in my arm and had to puncture me more than once.

When I was about ten and in hospital for yet another internal bleed into one of my joints, soon after the doctor had put up the daily drip and left for her rounds, my chest tightened, and I struggled to breathe. I hoarsely called the nurse hurrying past, but she was too pre-occupied to pay attention. "This is it," I thought, and resigned myself to the fact that I might be facing death. But just then my white-coated, eldest stepbrother Peter appeared. He was a medical student at the time and fortuitously popped in to see how I was doing. He immediately called the medics, who recognised an allergic reaction. I felt instant relief, the moment the antihistamine was injected.

A further significant breakthrough in hemophilia treatment came about in the early 1970s. A Canadian medical scientist discovered that the critical Factor VIII component could be skimmed off a pint of plasma, which separated into layers when it was spun at a very low temperature. The critical layer for bleeders, known as cryoprecipitate, is formed when frozen plasma is allowed to thaw slowly. It can then be freeze-dried and stored in a fridge at home.

So, since the mid-1970s, hemophiliacs can have their "Factor"—as we "Hemos" colloquially refer to Factor VIII—close at hand, and inject themselves intravenously when necessary or prophylactically, once or twice a week. This has been a life-changer, as it has obviated the need for long and protracted journeys to a Hemophilia Centre.

With the advent of home treatment an inevitable question among hemophiliacs is "How are your veins?" In my case, I have protruding veins on the top of my left hand but not on my right hand. This makes it convenient to insert the needle with my right hand; not that this is always successful, as sometimes I miss the vein altogether or go through it. Now that I am in my early seventies, I have developed scar tissue on my left hand, as a result of thousands of injections over my lifetime. This prompted a stranger on a train once to ask if I took recreational drugs.

While the concentrated factor was a huge boon for hemophilia treatment globally, the downside has been an increased risk of contamination, for example with Hepatitis B or Hepatitis C. The most consequential contaminant was the human immunodeficiency virus (HIV), which emerged in the mid-1980s, at a time when I was contemplating getting married. Ironically, being a privileged white South African exposed me to greater risk than my black hemophiliac counterparts. I had access to the expensive, imported concentrate factor, while they were on the home-produced cryoprecipitate. For them, the risk of contamination was almost zero as HIV was still extremely rare in South Africa then.

Today, Factor VIII is heat treated to eliminate contaminants. It can also be manufactured artificially in a laboratory, thereby ensuring that no contaminants are transfused but this is not yet generally available in South Africa. More significant is the fact that gene therapy has advanced to the stage where trials are currently being conducted as to the possibility of hemophilia being cured—at least in some patients.

AN HIV DIAGNOSIS

I had graduated with a law degree in 1976. After lawyering in Gauteng province for a decade, I decided to return to Cape Town where I registered for a postgraduate, multi-disciplinary degree in environmental studies at the University of Cape Town (UCT). I did this simply out of interest. Little did I know that it would lead to a riveting career path in environmental law, which would provide a lifeboat in some of the dark periods to follow.

I was living with my partner, Liz, while becoming immersed in ecological processes, geomorphology, and so on. We had both been reading in the popular press about a strange new disease affecting the three Hs: Homosexuals, Haitians, and Hemophiliacs. Later, a fourth H was added: Heroin addicts. I'd also heard something through the local hemophilia network about contaminated blood products. So, with Liz's encouragement, I decided, for peace of mind, to go and have myself tested for HIV at Tygerberg Hospital—the only place where the blood test was available at that time.

Dr Slabbert of the UCT Student Health office, who had taken a blood sample a few days previously, informed me that it would be better to fetch the blood-test results myself, rather than getting them from him, as originally arranged. The next day I arrived at the Pathology Laboratory building at Tygerberg Hospital and took the lift to the eighth floor. I recall that I was uncharacteristically on time, and that my heart was thumping. What is the room-number, I wondered?

Then a white-coated doctor appeared almost immediately at the door opposite the lift.

"Jan Glazeeeeew–?" He could not pronounce my surname.

I glanced behind him, down the long corridor with its Marley-tiled floor gleaming from that morning's scrubbing. "Glaze-EF-ski," I hesitatingly corrected him.

"You have AIDS," he said.

I stared at the cold smooth quartz tiles at the base of the hard face-brick walls.

I confronted the deep-down intuition I'd always had that the life-giving blood-clotting product would one day come back to bite me.

I was contaminated.

As I trudged back across the hot parking lot, I wondered what Liz's reaction would be; whether any woman would ever sleep with me again. Would I still be able to play with my dear friend Trish's kids? Maybe she and her husband Martin would not want me eating off their dinner plates.

I felt shell-shocked. I got back into my car and drove slowly back to UCT—there was seemingly nothing else that I could do. I shuffled back to my desk in an open plan office and mumbled to my classmate Bruce, "I have AIDS." I was not sure whether he heard, because he did not react, and we never mentioned it again. Even my aging father did not seem to register the earth-shattering news when I broke it to him—perhaps he did not want to hear.

Sometime later, I bumped into a bright young immunologist at Groote Schuur Hospital who had recently been appointed to head up a new HIV unit.

"Gary, tell me straight, how long have I got to live?"

"How old are you?" he asked.

"Thirty-two," I replied.

"Hmmm ... according to statistics, you have about four years to live," he responded matter-of-factly. Here I am, writing this four decades later.

"Why have I lived, while so many around me have died?" is a question I often ask myself.

DISCLOSING MY STATUS AND LIVING WITH HIV

Around the time that I was diagnosed HIV+, a Law Faculty advertisement crossed my desk for a Research Officer in the then Institute of Marine Law. Although not immediately appealing, after some investigation I realised that the post could accommodate my nascent passion for environmental law, in this case focussing on the coastline. This was a subject which was "struggling to be born in South Africa", accordingly to a legal luminary at the time. Immediately the picture changed for me.

Eventually, I received a letter in the post offering me the job but alarmingly, it was accompanied by a form that had to be completed by a medical doctor, certifying that I was in good health. I spent another few sleepless nights before consulting a local doctor to whom I disclosed my HIV status. He simply shrugged his shoulders, saying, "I'm sure it will be fine," and signed the form. The job was mine.

In the early 1990s, anti-retroviral (ARVs) drugs were generally not available and prohibitively expensive. While I was on a long-term work stint in Namibia, I often felt lethargic, with depleted energy levels. I sometimes wondered whether I would make the imminent millennium.

I learnt that the crucial markers were one's CD4 count, as well as the viral load. The former measures the state of one's immunity (normal is between 600 and 700 cells/mm3), while the viral load measures how much HI virus one is carrying. I returned from Namibia to learn that my viral load was over a million (copies/ml), while my CD4 count was perilously low—approaching 120, where one is regarded as having full-blown AIDS, rather than living with HIV.

So, in the late 1990s I started taking the powerful, most recently developed antiretrovirals (ARVs), commonly called the frontline drugs. I had to take various pills three times a day; some had to be crushed and tasted awful. They made me nauseous, and I became non-compliant.

The year 2000 saw Durban host the thirteenth International AIDS Conference. Coincidentally, the annual South African Law Teachers Conference was held in Durban at the same time. I had attended previous law conferences, and was tempted to go to the AIDS conference, but was once again in a dark period, feeling depressed. The thought of being in an alien environment and not knowing one person among the thousands there did not appeal. So, I attended the Law Teachers Conference instead.

Afterwards, I read in the press that at the opening event, eleven-year-old Nkosi Johnson, addressed the assembly in a moving description of how he was born HIV positive, and sought acceptance of his condition. Nkosi died the following year. When his adoptive mother disclosed that she had found his antiretroviral pills under the bed, I fully identified with him. He could not stand them, and I well understood why.

At that conference, Edwin Cameron, then Acting Judge of the Constitutional Court, gave an impassioned speech about living with HIV, stating that he was alive only because he could afford antiretroviral drugs, while tens of thousands could not. I drew great comfort from the fact that he publicly disclosed his status, and I gained confidence from that. Edwin became a role model for me.

ANTIRETROVIRAL DRUGS

At the time, my relationship with antiretroviral drugs was an unhappy one. Fortunately, I was referred to Dr Catherine Orrell, who was with the Desmond Tutu HIV centre at Groote Schuur Hospital. She was involved with clinical trials and the roll-out of HIV drugs in the townships. Upon meeting Catherine, I was immediately taken by her gentle, yet no-nonsense attitude.

I was anxious and depressed about my blood markers, and reluctant to continue the frontline drugs that I was taking half-heartedly, as they made me feel nauseous and light-headed. Catherine looked at me hard; then she drew the following sketch of a train approaching a cliff:

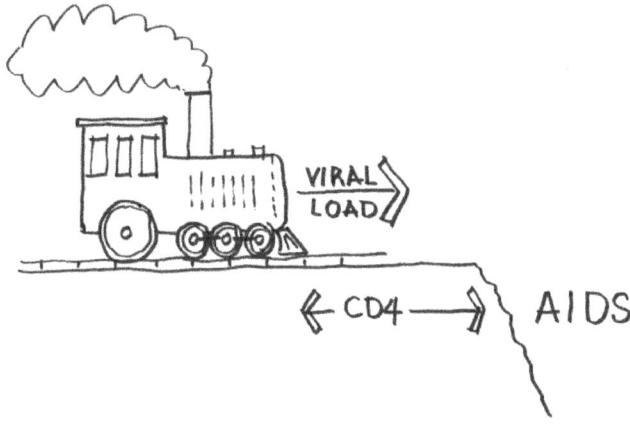

"The speed of the train is your HIV viral load," she announced. "The distance from the cliff is your CD4 count."

The depiction hit me like a thunderbolt.

The problem was that I had been dabbling with the frontline HIV drugs available on the market. The accepted view then was that if one had not been taking these frontline drugs properly, one would have built up a resistance, so there was no point in taking any previous standard drugs such as AZT. This was analogous to a chess game. The pawns were the standard drugs, which I had by-passed, and now I was playing with my knights, bishop and queen.

For a while, my cocktail included Nevirapine. Catherine said it would cause me to have vivid dreams, and encouragingly added that a Rastafarian patient of hers had stopped taking marijuana because the cocktail with Nevirapine was a good substitute. However, in my case the "vivid dreams" became hallucinatory, and so I stopped taking the drugs.

Catherine explained the various medical categories of drugs, which I struggled to get my head around: nucleoside reverse transcriptase inhibitors (NRTIs) that prevent HIV from replicating by blocking an enzyme called reverse transcriptase; and non-nucleoside reverse transcriptase inhibitors (NNRTIs) which prevent HIV from replicating by binding to and altering reverse transcriptase, which HIV uses to replicate. These reduce one's viral load.

Despite previously taking the frontline drugs, and having used up my bishops and knights, Catherine suggested trying the older, standard regime. She put me on a triple combination of AZT and 3TC with Efavirenz. "Let's see what happens," she said with a reassuring smile.

I had my levels checked again a month or so later, and when Catherine reported back on my blood tests, I was overjoyed to hear that my viral load had dropped dramatically and that my CD4 count had vastly improved. Catherine had managed not only to slow the train down, but also to push it back from the cliff. Since then, I have been permanently on ARVs and my viral load is undetectable, while my CD4 count is in the normal range.

I also became keenly involved in an interdisciplinary medical ethics group which met regularly at Groote Schuur Hospital. One day, the usual, austere meeting room was not available, so we met on an enclosed balcony high up, overlooking the Main Road in Observatory and the Cape flats beyond, where the poorer communities tended to live. I felt a slight headache as the white-coated doctors and other colleagues discussed, the issue of a HIV needle stick injury in the emergency room.

The white-coated doctor next to me seemed particularly animated, cutting into my thoughts . . .

"It's no longer a disease up in Africa," he proclaimed. "It's also a problem down there," gesturing towards the suburb of Observatory and the Cape Flats beyond.

I had an urge to tap him on the shoulder and whisper into his left ear: "It's actually sitting next to you, old chap . . . "

But I said nothing.

At the beginning of the following academic year, the convenor of the group asked all the members of the group to review their contributions to the group. I told them about my HIV status. It was quite a relief. My headaches seemed to subside after that.

Over time, I gathered up courage to disclose my status to more people and give talks on living with HIV, to the UCT community.

POSITIVITY IN ADVERSITY

In the early 1950s when I was born, hemophiliacs were not expected to have a normal life span. People ask me, "How come you've lived? What saved you?"

I have no definitive answer. I have survived due to a combination of factors: having the privilege of access to world-class medical treatment, meditation, psychotherapy, complementary therapies such as aromatherapy massage, a passion for my career, as well as physical exercise, particularly swimming, walking, riding an e-bike, and table tennis. In short, sheer bloody-mindedness.

But most of all, having supportive friends and a steadfast wife in later life, have seen me through. Lastly, I wonder if a fragment of my hemophiliac brother's spirit has permeated my being and urged me to live?

10

Living with Cluster Headaches

Bob Wold

Some forty-eight years ago, I was building my life, excited about my future as I began to start a family. I was in my mid-twenties, and a new home, young children and dreams were seemingly within reach. I remember the day and the exact time when my life changed. I remember the weather, the smells and feeling of fall in the air. I was playing football with my young son in my backyard. I began feeling a little sick with a slight pain starting to build on the side of my head. I felt the need to take a break, and I went inside to sit down.

Within minutes the pain had escalated far beyond anything I had ever experienced. The sharp, stabbing pain had begun in my right temple and quickly expanded to a burning pressure behind my right eye and traveled downward into my lower jaw and teeth. I would later describe it as "exquisite", as I searched for words that could adequately capture it. This pain knocked me off the couch and brought me to my knees, banging my head on the carpeted floor. As my wife and I contemplated calling an ambulance, I was about forty-five minutes into the attack when it dissipated, as quickly as it had come on.

What the hell was that? The pain had completely disappeared, and I looked for whatever damage it had caused and left behind. All that remained was the memory and resulting confusion. And a prayer that whatever it was would not return, ever. It did return. It has returned every year for forty-eight years.

When the attacks continued, we searched for answers. What was causing such pain and devastating life changes, and what could be done to end the suffering? Confounding everyone and delaying a correct diagnosis was the fact that the attacks would occur daily, multiple times per day, and would then stop rather suddenly after about six weeks.

Whichever new treatment I was currently using, we assumed to be the answer. When the attacks would return 6 months later, we would resume the previous treatment, but it would have no positive effect. The search began again.

Nothing helped. I have a vivid memory of driving my truck once when an attack was coming on. I pulled over to the side of the snow-covered road, wondering if popping out my eyeball would relieve the pain and pressure. I jumped from the truck and rammed my head into a snowbank, eating snow in the hope that ice would relieve the fire in my head. It didn't relieve anything.

I went through many treatment attempts. I had root canals performed on my teeth. When that didn't work, the teeth were pulled. After going through two of these six-week cycles every year for four years, I was finally given a CAT scan to see if I had a brain tumor. This pain had to be generated by something more serious than a sinus infection or toothache. The doctor came into the room and reported that there was no brain tumor. He smiled, thinking he was sharing good news, while my heart sank. I was looking for an answer, any answer. A tumor would have given me an answer and a path forward – no matter how difficult the road ahead of me, at least I would have had a road and map forward that would help me determine what needed to be done to end this agony. Was death now my only option?

Over those first four years of misdiagnosis, my "cycles" had increased in length to three months, and the number of attacks per day (and night) had increased to eight, with each lasting exactly an hour. I was finally referred to a local headache clinic. Five minutes into my appointment and after no more than five questions from the doctor, I was diagnosed with cluster headaches. This was the first time I had ever heard these words. If it was that easy to diagnose, why had it taken four years? This was also my first lesson in how much education was needed, directed toward the medical profession.

The following fifteen years were spent searching for an effective treatment. I tried over seventy different prescription medications in hundreds of combinations. If one medication seemed to offer even a 5% decrease in pain, I would not want to give it up, and we would add new medications. At one point I came out of the hospital on fifteen different prescription medications. None of them provided meaningful relief. The only thing that actually helped ease the pain was high-flow oxygen. My home and work were always full of large oxygen tanks. I have spent thousands of hours attached to an oxygen tank. A thirty-foot- (ten-meter)-long plastic tube allowed me to pace from the front to the back of my home as I counted the minutes until the pain would subside. The family would scatter, as they knew I didn't want them to witness such suffering. For caregivers this is a devastating disease as well, as they can't offer any aid to ease the pain, or even any comfort. I just needed them to get out of the way as I paced the floor.

The only living being who could stay with me was the family dog. She would actually come and sit across my feet before my attacks began—somehow, she knew when an attack was imminent. Lying across my feet guaranteed that she'd know when it was time to pace. She would pace with me, walking a couple of steps behind me, stepping to the side when I needed to turn around to pace back. When I'd finally stopped pacing and could collapse onto the couch, she'd again lie across my feet. I'll never forget that dog.

The dawn of the internet was life changing. I could do some research on headache conditions, but more importantly, I could meet other people suffering from the same malady. Like me, they often called the pain indescribable, or compared it to being stabbed in the eye with a red-hot ice pick. None of us were getting any answers from our doctors, and this new medium gave us a wider net to cast in search of answers. I had also met a couple of other cluster sufferers while in in-patient hospital settings getting treatment for my clusters. These meetings were short-lived as we checked into and out of the hospital, but to meet and speak with someone else who was going through the same devastating experience was in itself my most important treatment. When you suffer from something that no words can adequately describe, the human connection can substitute for words. You can try to explain that the broken ceramic tile on the shower wall is from banging your head, trying unsuccessfully to knock yourself out. This isn't an easy thing to try to explain to the people who love you. To another sufferer, all it takes is a nod of the head.

I was lucky enough to have a very supportive family and the support of close friends. Many people do not have that support. Even with a supportive community around you, these attacks are still nicknamed "suicide headaches". I have lost many a friend and acquaintance over the years to suicide.

Over the first twenty years of my journey with cluster headaches, I was able to build a life and family. Utilizing the pain-free time between cycles, and with the help of my wife, we were able to raise our children. I was able to hold a job by building a family business. My life had a positive change in the late 1990s due to the growing online community of "clusterheads" (as we're known). Since medical science was not of much help to us, we could exchange little bits of information that helped us get through the day, and even through life.

With several hundred of us gathered into an online community, we could find a supportive voice at any time during the day or night. If you found yourself contemplating suicide you could convey that fact without saying the words. We understood where you presently found yourself. Within minutes you would have a group coming to your aid. People knew if you just needed someone to listen, or for someone to call for emergency help. We were good at tracking people down in an emergency and sending local help to their door. You might have been in New Jersey at midnight and got help from someone in Australia. There was little distance among this community. For all the bad things that go on in the virtual world, there are also incredibly wonderful people quietly helping others.

One day, a young Scottish gentleman introduced himself to the online community and asked a simple question. As we were all accustomed to people sharing things that they found helpful, Flash, as he had come to be known, asked if anyone had heard of psychedelics as a possible effective cluster treatment. Some of the people were wondering if he was just trying to sell or score drugs. Others of us, always on the lookout for *anything* that might help, started to do a little research. Flash had shared what many of us had been sharing—anything that we felt had made a positive difference to our condition. He shared that his cluster cycle had not appeared at its usual time that fall, and the only thing he could determine that he'd done differently were a couple of recreational doses of LSD over the summer at rock concerts. A common occurrence within our group was that if we did anything that had either produced fewer or less severe attacks, we would repeat that action over and over in the hope of repeating the relief. If we had spaghetti for dinner the night before a good day with fewer attacks, we might have spaghetti for dinner every evening until our cycle ended.

Our research showed that LSD was discovered by a scientist who was also researching ergotamine, a substance used to treat headache disorders. We also found that some research, long buried, had been done with LSD and other psychedelics for headache disorders. This sparked an interest among several of us willing to investigate this possibility. LSD was hard to locate. None of us had much experience with psychedelics, even though many of us were children of the 1960s. A little more research showed us that psilocybin, found in magic mushrooms, was very similar to LSD on a molecular level. We also found that there was a way to grow these special mushrooms. We began our own community program of citizen science, and started growing our own medicine and testing it upon ourselves. We were a desperate group willing to try anything to find relief. Desperation is a powerful motivator.

The more we tested these theories upon ourselves, the more people were finding relief. Relief that wasn't offered by medical science, and in ways that current treatments couldn't even hope to achieve. Nothing available could end a normal cycle prematurely, nor prevent a cycle from happening according to its schedule. Psilocybin provided both of these benefits to more and more patients as we perfected the treatment regimen. I personally tried psilocybin in the middle of the worst cluster cycle of my life. Within an hour, my head was clear and empty of pressure, for the first time in years. Previous treatments may have temporarily tamped down the pain a bit, but always added a feeling of pressure. This was the first treatment that didn't leave me feeling "drugged up".

The biggest problem with getting access to these treatments was the illegality of psychedelics. Many people also would not try them due to their illicit status. People are programmed not to try anything that wasn't prescribed by their doctor and available at the local pharmacy. But for many, psychedelics became their last resort. Effective treatments are life-and-death decisions for people with cluster headaches. The pain of clusters will not kill you, but the psychological damage they cause has led thousands of people to take their own lives. Cluster headaches also cause everyone's physical health to deteriorate over the years. The decades of sleep deprivation, stress upon body and soul, and reduced sense of self-worth are devastating, both physically and psychologically.

It would have been easy, once finding an effective treatment, to happily go off and live a life we'd all been dreaming of for years. But this option was just not feasible to those of us in the community. We knew that we had to share this knowledge with others suffering as we had. The community was growing, but we knew that there were hundreds of thousands of people suffering who knew nothing of this possibility. We knew that someone's spouse or mother or father was currently considering suicide, unaware of this possible lifesaver. We also knew that even with this information, many people would not give it a try due to the lack of research and the illegality of the substance.

The need to push on in finding help for people in my community became a responsibility to continue to advocate, and to demand more research and the education of both patients and the medical community. Cluster headaches were poorly understood and, for the most part, ignored by those who could have been helpful in caring for people suffering such a fate.

My advocacy work has been both rewarding and frustrating. Having information that might provide meaningful help to others, brings with it a heavy burden, as does wanting to give people hope that they might not already have. I also encountered all the barriers set up by society to stop progress. But I also met many like-minded people with the same passion to help others, and this restored my faith in humanity every time that faith was tested.

This advocacy work became a serious responsibility for me, and also became an important part of my own treatment program. Helping others and righting some of society's wrongs gave me a sense of purpose, a reason to go on when reasons were hard to find.

Psychedelics had been put on the shelf for forty to fifty years, yet we were far behind on research. We had found something that could possibly ease the suffering of millions of people worldwide, that was currently illegal and said to have no medical purpose. Where was the nearest mountaintop from which I could shout this?

I therefore formed Clusterbusters as a non-profit dedicated to getting research underway as soon as possible. We needed respected voices within the medical community to prove our findings for several reasons. One was to show the establishment that, yes, psychedelics can work to treat pain, and another was to let the public know that science has proved their effectiveness, and you don't need to take the word of a faceless person on the internet telling you to take psychedelics to treat one of the most painful conditions known to medicine.

I enlisted a couple of people from the community to help, and one of them was kind enough to provide seed funding. Eventually we were able convince a group of Harvard Medical researchers of the need for research on psychedelics for the treatment of cluster headaches. There were still daily obstacles, but in 2006, our first research was published, four years after forming Clusterbusters and eight years after I first tried psilocybin for my cluster headaches.

In the years since, we have made big strides in educating the medical profession and governmental healthcare agencies about cluster headaches. Many people and media outlets want to know who these people are who are taking psychedelics, and the most dramatic part of the story always ends up being about cluster headaches and not psychedelics.

Capitalism has not been a friend to people with cluster headaches. There are approximately 350,000 people in the USA who have been diagnosed with clusters. But there are too many people to qualify for "orphan drug" status to finance research for new treatments, and too few people to interest the pharmaceutical industry—especially with a non-patentable natural substance so effective that you may only need a couple of pills every year.

Advocacy work is what has saved my life and given it a passionate purpose. We are always our own best advocate, but it is a small step, going from personal advocacy to advocating for an entire community. We each know what we need. It's just a matter of changing the words from "I need" to "we need."

11

Living with a Heart Transplant

Evance Kalula

THE BEGINNINGS

It has been over thirty years since I had the privilege of coming to the shores of the "Cape of Good Hope." My lived experience since then has been a rich one, both in adversity with the challenges it has brought and continues to bring, and opportunities that have been profound.

Adversity is inherent in the human condition. It inevitably brings with it tribulations that often are difficult to comprehend, not least the opportunities that it generates in its train. The main and overriding adversity I have had to deal with has been in relation to my health.

When I reflect on the beginnings, the irony of experience is that it is the adversity of my health that in essence sent me on the path of opportunities that I have been privileged to enjoy. It could in fact be said that my survival itself originated from that initial health adversity I came to face.

It all started for me in Luanshya, Roan Antelope Mines on the Zambian Copperbelt, seventy-three years ago. My dear father was a miner with a rare foresight. The miner's lot was not a walk in the park. It was a hard life, but despite that it was seen as a relatively fortunate life, one that provided for families in relative comfort and devoid of the abject poverty of the rural areas. Not surprisingly, every miner's son looked forward to that life, to stepping into their father's shoes. The mines obliged. Most miners' sons were assured of jobs along with or in succession to their fathers. That was the unwritten but honoured deal.

Uncharacteristically, my father had serious reservations. Although he had faithfully laboured as one, he knew the high cost of a miner's work. He had been a victim of silicosis, reassigned to lighter work, and later 'pensioned' off with a watch as a token. That came later, but earlier he had resolved that he would strive to assist any son of his who wanted out of that life.

And there I was, sickly with a weak chest, with later speculation that I might have been one of the many victims of the emission from the smelters that covered the mine "native townships" with perpetual smog. As if that were not enough, I was bookish, attracted to the unknown mysteries that books seemed to hold. The stage was set. I have no recollection of how exactly it happened, but the result is that I was sent back to my mother's village and subsequently entered the Dutch Reformed Church missionary school's system that was to prove my deliverance.

I never totally got over my weak chest, but in time it improved with country air, so much so that by the time I got to university, I was quite active in some sports, considered to have both the intellectual and physical attributes adequate to be elected Rhodes scholar for the then combined constituency of Rhodesia and Zambia in 1975. And so, I got to my beloved Balliol College. I was good enough at some sports, including hockey (eventually earning half-blue in it at Oxford), golf and squash. However, health concerns later came back to haunt me. The adversity intensified; it almost took me to death's door.

ONSET OF ADVERSITY

The impending decline in my health started when I relocated to the Kingdom of Lesotho in the late 1980s. I had taken up an appointment teaching at the National University Lesotho (NUL). It was a rejuvenating opportunity to go back to academic work after a number of uncertain years at the International Labour Organization (ILO) in Geneva, and then completing my PhD, which had been interrupted for almost five years.

The health adversity that later confronted me in Lesotho was not immediate; it was progressive and did not really set in until 1990. By the time I moved to Cape Town in 1992, the symptoms of what was later diagnosed as heart failure were more pronounced. The cause of the condition itself was not clear and has never really been pinned down. Could it have been due to rheumatic fever that was not adequately treated in childhood, complicated by asthma, or did the Lesotho's high altitude accelerate it?

The onset leading to the dramatic turn of events I discuss below was progressive. I had always led an active life, notwithstanding that I was no longer active in sport. I became more lethargic, constantly overcome by fatigue. Routine activities became more cumbersome. That deterioration was more evident in a number of ways, including occasional shortness of breath after what usually was normal exertion. It got worse, to a point where I could not tie my shoes laces; it subsequently led to my abandoning my brogues, to which I had become accustomed as a symbol of well-togged feet.

My health challenges came to the fore on 26 June 2002. It was dramatic. I suffered a stroke in the early hours of the morning on that fateful day. Up to that time, I had settled down quite well despite the onset of the symptoms I have referred to above, except for the occasional seasonal colds and flu. Although my condition was stabilised with chronic medication, from then onwards my health became more uncertain, and the impact on my wellbeing was drastic. It impinged on my life in various ways, both physically and psychologically. While I more or less came to terms with the physical challenges of my condition, the psychological effects were more difficult to deal with. My confidence was progressively eroded, depression set in, life became a struggle it had never been. I was afraid of what it might lead to.

ROAD TO SURVIVAL AND SUPPORT

My journey in the face of adversity, apparently in the quest for redemption and survival, has been and continues to be remarkable. I would not have reached this stage of the journey without the support of many people and groupings. The first of such sources of support through affirmation and unconditional love has been my immediate and wider family. My dear wife Sebastiana and our children, Kabuswe Kenneth, Twanji Joseph, Olipa Kunda and Musindosi Natasha, have simply been incredible.

Apart from family support, I have been fortunate to have an outstanding medical team and caregivers, as well as friends and a fraternity of fellow survivors' support group. The first of these was my cardiologist, Dr Adrian Horak. I became Dr Horak's patient when I suffered the stroke in 2002. He was instrumental in not only ensuring that I recovered from the stroke, but in giving me hope for longer survival. For the following ten years, Dr Horak cared for me, many times beyond the call of duty. It reached a point when the condition seemed irreversible. He persuaded me to join the transplant waiting list. As I have mentioned above, the chronic medication stabilised my condition somewhat, but the constraints were pronounced. Dr Horak tried to intervene with the latest medication management techniques available to him. Incidentally, his intervention happened to be world class, fortunately reflecting South Africa's continuing ability to maintain its place as a pioneer in cardiology. As a patient, I felt the limitation of that intervention. I was not getting any better; my ability to carry out normal activities continued to deteriorate, my mental health also being adversely affected.

When the fateful day came, with total heart failure, a donor was fortunately found that enabled me to have the heart transplant on 19 December 2012. The transplant team, headed by Dr Willie Koen, with Dr Otto Thanning as my bedside attending surgeon, was remarkable. The other care givers, in particular Helena Williams, the Transplant Coordinator, initially Karin Tilney, team Occupational Therapist, and later Yvonne Gärtner, transplant team Clinical Neuropsychologist, were and continue to be "angels on earth."

Although I was vaguely aware of the impending transplant, I did not fully internalise it until after I had gone through it and was in the Intensive Care Unit (ICU). It eventually dawned on me what had happened. I was in turmoil with a swell of emotions going through me. As Dr Otto Thaning, my attending surgeon, explained to me that I had a heart transplant and assured me that all would be well, I was momentarily relieved but later confused. As I lay there watching the monitors, with an external pacemaker supporting my new heart before it took over to function on its own, anxiety set in. Long after I was discharged from hospital, when I asked Dr Thaning if he ever doubted my recovery, his categorical response was that he did not, as he had watched countless patients go through the same anxiety.

After I was discharged and on track to recovery, new anxieties emerged: a great sense of guilt that someone else had to die for me to be alive. I was regularly gripped with a recurring nightmare, in which my supposed donor was dying from an accident and his heart was wrenched from his chest in the ambulance, at which point I woke up in great distress. It was later explained to me that my nightmare was due to a baseless sense of guilt.

It was further explained that my donor had not died from an accident, and that "he" was in fact "she."

And so, my journey to full recovery continued with multiple medications, significant among them, immuno-suppressants. Lifesaving as the medications have been, they have been a source of various challenges. I have had to adjust to a strict regime of compliance with the adverse side effects they entail, namely making me more prone to opportunistic infections that linger on much longer.

The adversity that comes with conditions such as heart transplant and the aftermath, need support beyond family, medical care, and friends. Solidarity from fellow survivors, and dedicated organizations such as the Organ Donor Foundation (ODF), have also been crucial. They have not only been there for me, but also encouraged me to reach out to others. The role of the ODF has been significant; it continues to educate and encourage the public to become organ donors. It is not an easy task to persuade the public to be organ donors. Not only is it ill timing to ask family in mourning to let their loved ones to be generous in that unique way, but there are also deeply entrenched cultural and religious constraints. The ODF's work is therefore highly commendable in that it continues to increase awareness.

A number of other individuals and groups have also been invaluable and helped me in the face of adversity. The late Stanley Henkelman and his wife Sharon, and Hermann and Lyn Steyn, were incredible role models. Stanley, an athlete of distinction who, until his untimely death, was a world Transplant Games one-hundred metres record holder, was a great inspiration not only to fellow survivors but also as ambassador at large. 'Big brother' Hermann, who had his transplant just before mine, symbolised fraternal courage in the face of adversity. Sadly, both fell victim to the onslaught of the COVID-19 pandemic, as did many other transplant survivors.

The "New Hearts and LVAD Family" support group has been, and continues to be, another remarkable source of mutual encouragement and inspiration. The group provides a platform for both survivors and those waiting to have various organ transplant surgery. Two fellow heart transplant survivors, Anthony Breakey and Ray Hartley, with their respective wives, Chantal and Belinda, have particularly been indispensable sources of mutual encouragement and support in the face of adversity.

Faith, in both the religious and broader spiritual sense, has always played a central part in my life, particularly during my formative years. As I have indicated above, I am a product of missionary schools of the Dutch

Reformed Church. Although the intensity of my adherence to faith in practice has varied over the years, it has always defined and guided my outlook. That faith has been crucial in facing up to my health challenge, both before and after my transplant. I was privileged to be sustained by the support of the Kloof Street Cape Peninsula Reformed Congregation (CPRC), first under Dr Francois Wessels and later, Reverend Arion Naidoo.

Beyond the CPRC congregation, I have found solace in the affirmation of a remarkable fraternity, the Living Causes of Life Initiative (LCLI). The initiative, was led by Gary Anderson and Teresa Cutts from Wake Forest University, North Carolina. The convener of LCLI is Jim Cochrane, emeritus professor of religious studies at the University of Cape Town (UCT). With the support of his theologian wife Renate, he has done remarkable work to harness the common cause of an outstanding group of like-minded people, and he kindly drew me into it. The idea of LCLI denotes the affirmation of "leading causes of life", in contrast to the "leading causes of death" narrative. It has undoubtedly broadened my spiritual outlook and reflections; it has alerted me to the complexity of the relationship between life and wellbeing. It has thus been of great assistance in helping me face up to my health adversity.

FACING DIVERSITY AT THE UNIVERSITY OF CAPE TOWN

This account of living with a heart transplant would not be complete without reference to the adversity experienced at my place of work, UCT, both before and after my transplant. The experience I encountered after my transplant was traumatic both emotionally and physically, and directly related to living with a heart transplant. Two instances in particular illustrate this experience, but I must emphasize that this took place against the backdrop of an otherwise fulfilling and positive experience at UCT.

I found my colleagues at the Faculty of Law, and later at the International Academic Programmes Office (IAPO), supportive. Besides, UCT as my employer was kindly accommodating, and assisted with my adjustment to cope with my health challenge. I am most indebted to the University's policies and senior management.

I was also fortunate to be Warden of Kopano Residence. The student residence system at UCT appealed to both my aspirations about the changes needed towards true transformation beyond race and class, and my lived experience of relating to people from various backgrounds. It is central to my personal philosophy and belief in "our common humanity in diversity."

I therefore found being Warden of Kopano a very gratifying position. I spent most of my formative years in boarding institutions from when I was very young. I could therefore relate to my wards. In that respect I easily took on the role of guardian and mentor as a "labour of love," a trait which has endured to this day.

The situation however drastically and suddenly changed with the onset of the "Rhodes Must Fall" agitation in 2015. Although I had been fortunate to overcome most of the physical effects of my heath adversity, the protests brought forth an uncertain and unsettling time, not least because I was inexplicably one of the targets. The dynamics of the ethos of "cooperative governance" that the UCT student residences evoked were abandoned in the face of uncertain goals. I came under siege both physically and psychologically in the environment that came to prevail. It was very traumatic. What also heavily weighed on me is the fact that I was in part targeted on account of being a heart transplant beneficiary. I was made to feel, and was told, that undergoing a heart transplant was somehow not in keeping with "ancestral call and wishes" to join them. It was seen as contrary to "African culture and traditional values."

Besides the hostile atmosphere that overtook the residences, my adversity was worsened by the attitude of my new line management at IAPO, which more or less coincided. With hindsight, I think that the coincidental unfolding of the developments was the beginning of the storm that later overwhelmed the University. Although the situation still reverberates, that is another story. I feel I have to mention it in passing. It was a significant factor in the adversity I endured; it was therefore part and parcel of what it meant to live with a heart transplant. My experience was very traumatic and heightened the sense of adversity. I was fortunate to retire just as these events were unfolding.

QUEST FOR LABORS OF LOVE AND REDEMPTION

And what does all this mean? The human condition and experience present an incredible enigma. Given the destructive tendencies of humans towards each other, often signified by endless conflicts and denial of our common humanity, not to mention our reckless dereliction of duty of care towards our habitat, is it surprising that some would question our right to continue to be custodians of our planet? And yet the same species is capable of remarkable good. Through ingenuity and innovation, means to improve, and above all, save lives bare testimony to that capability. I have been fortunate to be a beneficiary of that enlightened side of human endeavour. It has enabled me to face my health adversity through an extension of my tenancy on earth, to pursue labours of love and continue to seek my redemption, elusive as the latter might be.

At times, fortunately rare, when I am seized by delusions of inexplicable grandeur, I am reminded of the words of King Alphonso X the Learned: "Had I been present at the creation, I would have given some useful hints for the better ordering of the universe." It is absurd that anyone, even His Learned Majesty, would ever contemplate being present at the creation of such a complex phenomenon that humanity is. For me, I count my blessings that I was not featured in that ordering at all; the best I can do is "search for redemption" by giving back to humanity as much as I can, in pursuing labours of lave and what could be said is "uncertain redemption."

And so, it has come to pass, fate has been kind to me, I think adversity and opportunity are more closely linked than is realised. One could add that the two "would eventually account for themselves, our role should be to endeavour to share the lived experience they bring forth." The link has been fortunate for me; it has enabled me to face up to health adversity and make good on the opportunities that have come my way. It could be said that in the midst of health challenges, the phenomena of adversity and opportunity have spared me. I feel fortunate; fate has been kind to me. As Stanlake Samkange, the late Zimbabwean historian and novelist might have said: "I am glad I stopped on these shores of the Cape of Good Hope!"

12

Living with (premature) Menopause

Cansu Özge Özmen

ALTHOUGH MY CHILDHOOD WAS not completely trauma free, I was in no hurry to grow up. Adulthood, from what I could gather, seemed to be full of tedious responsibilities; old age was even worse, personified by an elderly aunt of my mother's, as a time for silent prayers, frequent walks to the bathroom, a state of holding on—to walls, canes, other people, and life.

I remember the first time I heard the song in which Orson Welles, addressing a young person, says: "I know what it is to be young, but you, you don't know what it is to be old". I thought the lyrics were dumb. The singer, to my mind, clearly had no advantage in knowing what it was to be old. The much-celebrated wisdom came at such great costs, that I would rather not have it.

Still, when I was 15 and was the only student in my class who had not gotten her period, I was very frustrated. Surely there was something wrong with me. When my best friends went to the bathroom to change their pads and told me about how they bled, I was fascinated and jealous. When our biology teacher told us during class that having one's period was nothing to be ashamed of and that it was a sign of good health, I immediately demanded to be taken to a gynecologist. Everything seemed to be in order, the doctor said. I was just a late bloomer.

I got my period the next year. We celebrated with a cake. It did not take me long to realize the last time I would be thrilled to see that fresh, pinkish stain would be the first time. I was thinking it would have been better never to have bloomed at all. It was painful, disgusting, and mostly uncomfortable.

During that time, I came across a quote about old age, sometimes attributed to Maurice Chevalier: "Old age isn't so bad when you consider the alternative". That's the first time it really struck me that whatever I wished or not wished about becoming an adult, getting my period, aging, or whether I bloomed early or late, were insignificant. There really were two alternatives—ageing and death. Both were inevitable, and I had relatively no control over either. Having a period at least meant that I was still relatively young. It was just that youth involved pain and discomfort too, in other ways.

Twenty-two years later, I stopped having periods after my first dose of adjuvant chemotherapy. But I did not mind it, for a few reasons. I was in survival mode and had other side effects to worry about. As I did not wish to give birth, I was not concerned about infertility. And I certainly could use some time off from PMS and cramps.

The oncologist told me that sometimes menstruation came back once the treatment was over. But because of the type of tumor I had, I would have to get medication to induce premature menopause. Later we found out that I had a breast cancer gene mutation, BRCA1, which increases the risk of breast cancer as well as ovarian cancer and in varying degrees other types of cancers. So, after months of adjuvant chemotherapy, and HER2 inhibitor targeted therapy, I went through three surgeries: two mastectomies, and one total hysterectomy with bilateral salpingo-oophorectomy. I was 38, and I was in surgically induced premature menopause. Overnight, which is the only kind when you get a surgically induced menopause.

The first thing I realized was how little the doctors seemed to know or care about menopause. When I shared some of my concerns and told them about the recent changes in my body, their response was that they were natural, expected, and there wasn't much one could do to address those issues. On one occasion, after telling my gynecologist how painful sexual intercourse was, he told me it was completely normal, and that at one point I would have difficulty controlling my bladder, too. Thus, menopause, to me, was not a gradual transition into the age of wisdom. It was not a new season, when one slowed down and learned to enjoy what life would now offer to one's mature self. Not all of its symptoms were temporary. I could lose some of the fundamental functions of my body. I had already left behind a few organs. And now I had heart palpitations, shortness of breath, insomnia, osteoporosis, general weakness, vaginal dryness, eye dryness, and slowed metabolism; symptoms and states I have never experienced before in my life.

Eye dryness, compared to others, does not seem to be a very dramatic symptom. After all, you can use artificial tears to ease the discomfort. But eye dryness also causes blurry vision, light sensitivity, and pain. You need to wear sunglasses in the daytime or else the sunlight is blinding; you need to wear blue-light blocking glasses when you are looking at screens; sometimes you cannot see clearly, no matter what glasses you wear; your eyes get really tired despite using artificial tears, and you can feel your eyelids rub against your eyes, which is painful. Suddenly, you need all this paraphernalia, none of which can eradicate the problems. Now you need lubricant to have sex, eye drops to see, heart medication to slow down the heartbeats, a diet list to maintain optimal weight, vitamins to boost your energy. And there is a whole market out there full of useless but nonetheless tempting products to relieve you of your menopausal symptoms.

I could not receive hormone replacement therapy because of the type of tumor I had, as estrogen could cause my cancer to metastasize. Sometimes doctors would imply that symptoms of menopause were negligible when compared with what I had gone through during treatment. But the treatment was saving my life. Menopause, on the other hand, did not strike me as purposeful. You bear the surgeries and the chemotherapy because you want to stay alive; you bear the menopause, and it foretells your decline.

The second thing that struck me was my own ignorance about the matter. I realized not many people really talk about menopause, just like they did not tell children much about what to expect before they get their period. To make matters worse, the usual source of information about periods, kissing, masturbation, herpes, or any other new experience was not available. My peers could not help me at all. Once again, I was the only one of my peers not having her period.

Shortly after the hysterectomy, I was prescribed another medication to suppress the estrogen secreted by the adrenal glands. That's when all the previous symptoms such as the hot flashes, sudden bouts of anger, difficulty sleeping, weight gain, low libido faded in comparison. For lack of a better expression, I became an old person. I did not get old. Getting somewhere implies a journey, a process. I became old. So now, I was relatively young, and I also partially knew what it was to be old, minus the wisdom.

I do not mean to imply natural perimenopausal or menopausal (as opposed to surgically induced premature menopausal) symptoms, some of which I have experienced, are not challenging. The symptom that the general public seems to be most familiar with, hot flashes, does not result from being exposed to intense heat. There is no external source of heat that gradually raises your temperature. It feels like a sudden fire inside your (at least in my) head. Or like your brain has been boiling for a while, and suddenly you regain consciousness and start feeling the heat. It's like your body's thermostat is broken and the temperature keeps fluctuating. I learned to tolerate it, of course. It happens often enough, but at first, I had to stop whatever I was doing. A splash of cold water, fanning, and air conditioning do not really help. The cold you apply externally cannot put out the internal fire. Duration and frequency vary. You can never be prepared for it. You can be in the middle of a conversation, an interview, an official dinner. Once it's gone, as it departs as suddenly as it arrives, you get the impression that it must show; there must be some third-degree burns on your face. But there usually is no sign, except for a pinkish hue. Then I started to try to work through it, keep on reading, writing, walking through it. I cannot say it helped, but it gives me a sense of purpose, an illusion of resistance.

Once all the estrogen I could produce was suppressed, I started feeling much weaker. Most of the time, I had difficulty distinguishing between the after-effects or side effects of chemotherapy, surgeries, the medications I was on, and menopause. At first, I refused to believe I could not live as I had always lived. Heat never bothered me before. I could walk for miles under the sun. I could stay up all night reading and still be functional the next day. I could drink as much coffee as I wanted and fall asleep the minute my head touched the pillow. I could have an argument without having a nervous breakdown. I did not scream at bad drivers. I did not cry for hours because a friend of mine stopped being vegan. I could remember people's birthdays. I could remember what I went into the kitchen for. I could remember whom I was calling while listening to the phone ringing in my ear. I could sit cross-legged and could walk without limping when I stood up. I could concentrate. I could get out of bed without doing stretching exercises.

It turns out it was not just my eyes that had dried up. It was my whole body. Apparently, estrogen is vital for the musculoskeletal function. It decreases stiffness in ligaments and joints. That's exactly how my whole body felt: stiff. When my joints did not ache, I felt like a wooden puppet, with as much flexibility. I had so much pain in my knees that I started thinking I would need a new pair if I was to live for more than a decade.

After some psychotherapy, and a new antidepressant prescription, I had to accept that I must adapt to this new, strange version of myself. I would alleviate the symptoms I could alleviate through exercise and herbal supplements. During a walk one noontime, I got so weak that my friend had to carry me back to the car. I also started crying uncontrollably because I was embarrassed. But carrying me also proved very difficult because my breast implants hurt, my surgical wound hurt, and he did not know how to hold me in his arms. Resistance was exhausting. And useless. I would have to walk at nights and use the daytime for grieving for my old self.

Another symptom that I denied for as long as I could, and one that probably bothered me the most, was cognitive dysfunction. In retrospect, maybe the decline also undermined my denial mechanism. I teach for a living, and I have been teaching more or less the same courses for the past fourteen years. I have taught through four months of chemotherapy with no obvious sign of difficulty, but now I felt like everyone could see how many words escaped me, how many titles of books were completely erased from my mind, how many sentences were left unfinished because I could not remember how I began them. Simple conversations became frustrating since I had to make an effort just to remember the question I asked as I listened to the person respond to my question.

On the upside, I could not argue with anyone anymore, since I did not have any train of thought. I had independent compartments that did not make sense on their own. I had heard about chemo brain, I knew anesthesia could cause cloudy thinking, and one of the symptoms of menopause is brain fog. All the other symptoms of menopause also have an impact on cognitive function. If you cannot sleep well, you cannot think well. If you are burning inside, you cannot concentrate properly. If your mood constantly changes, it is hard to maintain a sufficient amount of motivation to do anything. So, you can never quite discern the intricacies of interrelated symptoms.

Brain fog is a very befitting term, as I felt like I could only participate in conversations, classes, arguments, and life in general, through a dense fog. I could make out the silhouettes and lights, but I had to drive really slowly not to crash into anything. Just as I thought I had figured out what I was facing, it turned out to be something completely different. I was often misunderstood because I could not express myself clearly enough, and I frequently misunderstood people because I found it easier to reach my own conclusions than to focus on what they were trying to tell me. I realized however, that I also felt less anxiety. Perhaps I could not muster the mental energy to come up with scary scenarios about the future. I spent all of it on day-to-day survival skills.

They say the first year is the hardest, and it was. Today, a year and a half later, I have much less frequent hot flashes, more physical energy, and my brain feels more misty than foggy. I still have a hard time falling asleep after exhausting all the available meditations and sleep exercises and listening to white, brown, and pink noises online, to no avail. Watching cats sleep, and listening to boring audiobooks sometimes help. When the books are spellbinding, they have the opposite effect. Every time I get up, I hesitate. I have had a few falls, because I overestimated my knees' carrying capacity. It certainly is a time for discovery, a discovery of the limitations of my new body. Or rather, my old body.

People seem to think that induced premature menopause is a small price to pay to continue living cancer-free. It is a price I would pay a hundred times over, but the fact that I would eventually —albeit gradually—become menopausal anyway, or the fact that the surgery decreased the risk for more primary cancers to a great extent, and metastasis to some extent, does not render it inconsequential. People also seem to expect me, or any other person in my condition, to be grateful for the relatively small price paid to lower our risk for another bout of cancer and not make a big deal out of it.

The fact that I or any other woman eventually and inevitably becomes menopausal is no consolation at all. Whether it comes sooner or later, menopause is an unpleasant experience. I am happy for those who can find meaning and joy in inevitable adversities, those who come out stronger and more confident on the other end, those who use menopause for self-discovery, and build a better self.

Unfortunately, I am not one of them. Even if I were a better or stronger person today than I was before menopause, it still was a very unpleasant process imposed on me by circumstances out of my control. I would have preferred to become a better or stronger person by making a conscious decision. I am overjoyed because treatments and induced premature menopause have (probably) extended my life, but my joy does not provide me with immunity against lesser kinds of pain and suffering. Besides, I think the inadvertent pressure to be and remain grateful lays an additional burden on the person who is going through any kind of adversity, including menopause.

Denial, resistance, sadness are not processes I went through because I was not aware that there were worse conditions to be in. I could and still can clearly remember the pre-menopausal version of myself. So, I was aware both of the facts that there was a version of myself who suffered less, and an imaginary version of myself who could suffer more. I could grieve, bid farewell to an intact, stronger self, but that does not mean I would stop hoping my life did not take such a sudden turn. Both cancer and premature menopause shattered an illusion I had about myself. I was a late bloomer, and I would also be a late witherer. And I miss myself being in full blossom. I know what it is to be young, and I wish I could have stayed young a while longer.

13

Living with Parkinson's Disease

Denis Daneman

I AM A SEVENTY-FIVE-YEAR-OLD man, South African-born and schooled, trained and worked for over forty years as a pediatric endocrinologist in Toronto, Canada, married more than fifty years, father of two sons, grandfather of three, and now retired. I have had Parkinson's disease for almost eighteen years.

On a Sunday morning in October 2006, I woke my wife and said simply: "I have Parkinson's Disease" (PD). "How do you know?" she asked, surprised. I gave her the same answer I subsequently gave, on 16 November, when I saw a movement disorders neurologist for the first time: "I have ruled out all the alternatives."

Symptoms had started about eight months earlier. At first, I attempted to ignore them, attributing my crushing exhaustion, insomnia, intermittent (and at times vigorous) tremor of my left hand, to the stresses and strains of applying for a prestigious new position with ramped up responsibilities. I didn't understand the significance of a comment made to me along the way by a nursing colleague: "Why does your left arm not swing like the right when you walk?" It turns out that this is a well-recognized feature of PD.

As the symptoms progressed, being a physician, I went through the differential diagnosis of serious neurologic disorders, ruling out, in order, ALS (Lou Gehrig's Disease), multiple sclerosis, then Alzheimer's, and was left with the most obvious: PD. No blood work needed, an MRI performed, and the diagnosis confirmed clinically. No chance of going back. And I learned very quickly that PD is devoid of any redeeming features. There certainly is no entertainment value.

By this time, I had been offered and accepted the role of Professor and Chair of the Department of Paediatrics, University of Toronto, and Paediatrician-in-Chief at The Hospital for Sick Children (SickKids). My first question to my neurologist was: "Does this mean I should resign from my positions?" "Absolutely not," he said. "I have patients who are judges, lawyers, physicians, literally from all walks of life, who continue functioning at the highest levels despite PD." A few of my colleagues were less forgiving and hinted that I might not be up to the task.

One of the biggest unknowns about PD is that there are no indicators which can be used to predict the course of the disease. Progression varies from very slow to quite rapid.

So, I approached my two "bosses" with the news. Both the hospital CEO and the University Dean were extremely supportive and agreed that I should continue in my new roles until or unless the burden of PD came to interfere with my functioning. Of that part of my story, the outcome is now known: I completed the maximum allowed two five-year terms, with great support from the university and hospital. The best recognition of my performance came in 2017 when I was made an Officer of the Order of Canada, the country's highest civilian honour, for my contributions to child health and diabetes care in Canada. I must confess to having dozed off many times during the endless meetings associated with the job.

An aside: I should add that from the time of diagnosis of PD, every time I have been given an award or honour, I would always say the same thing to my wife: "All very nice, but it does not cure PD." A good deal of the joy of these sorts of events was damped down by the PD. The sense of loss was and remains pervasive. Moreover, these awards were recognition of past contributions, water under the bridge.

But let me go back to the time of diagnosis. I knew quite a lot about PD, and more than a handful of people with the disease. I knew that PD is a chronic neurodegenerative disorder, with an unrelenting course. The time course varies greatly, and my tremor-predominance offered a better (that is, slower) time course of deterioration than those who present with predominant stiffness. There were no simple diagnostic tests for the condition or treatments that led to a cure or even slower progression.

Living with Adversity

Like many other chronic conditions, claims of breakthroughs in PD are not uncommon. One learns to be sceptical of these. In fact, the mainstay of treatment remains the tried and tested L-Dopa-Carbidopa (brand name Sinemet) combination, plus some adjunctive therapies. Sinemet has been in use since even before I was a medical student in the 1960s to 1970s. Promises of better treatments were fueled by some success with deep brain stimulation and possibly also stem cell research. The signs and symptoms are many and varied. I thought the usually described main symptoms—stiffness, masklike faces, festinant gait (shuffling walk), and pill-rolling tremor—were the ones most likely to interfere with daily living. Not so: insomnia, daytime exhaustion, bowel dysfunction, soft voice, and mood disturbance, have caused more problems.

The major aspects of PD management included maintenance of an appropriate body weight with physical activity and diet. Although there are PD-specific exercise routines, such as BIG (a description of the type of movements done), any exercise is considered worthwhile. Escalating medications in order to minimize symptoms. Side-effects of the medications include troubling dyskinesias (uncontrolled movements), excessive food intake, compulsive gambling, and heightened sexuality. My weight has fluctuated somewhat, but most side-effects have been absent. Adjunctive therapies are added when needed—for balance issues, gastrointestinal and mood symptoms, for example.

My daily pill routine provides the most relentless reminder of having PD, having evolved steadily to a grand total of twenty-two pills administered at six or seven time points each day:

- At around 7 a.m. or 8 a.m. I take two Levo-Dopa-Carbidopa, three Pramipexole, two Rasagaline and one amantadine (8 tablets).
- At about 11 a.m., two more Levo-Dopa-Carbidopa (2 tablets).
- Between noon and 1 p.m., three more Pramipexole and one Amantadine (4 tablets).
- At 3 p.m. or 4 p.m., two more Levo-Dopa-Carbidopa (2 tablets).
- At 6 p.m. or 7 p.m., three Pramipexole, one Amantadine (4 tablets)
- Between 10 p.m. and 11 p.m., two more Levo-Dopa-Carbidopa (2 tablets)

Remembering to take the pills is easy. If I miss the pills, the symptoms of PD quickly become amplified. The annual cost of these medications is exorbitant but is almost entirely covered by my ongoing medical insurance plan. Chalk one up for the Canadian health care system!

I recall helping an older colleague with PD to start a similar medication routine. He had advanced neurodegeneration and just could not "get" the routine I was trying to describe, even after I wrote it down very carefully. The responsibility for medication administration had to be put on the shoulders of his care providers. Unfortunately, he died shortly thereafter, having sustained further brain injury in a fall down a flight of stairs. This served as a grim warning of what the future might hold.

FOUR VIGNETTES

1. Staying at the front

At the time of diagnosis of PD, my neurologist was talking to me about a (randomized controlled) trial of a new medication that, in preliminary studies, was felt to offer neuroprotection in PD, and that would slow down the rate of neurodegeneration. The trial had just finished recruiting subjects. It would be another two to three years before the results would be known. Not keen to wait so long, I asked my physician whether the drug was approved for use in other situations by the federal regulatory body. "Yes, and it has an excellent safety profile," he answered. Then I said: "Please prescribe it for me, on the understanding that there may be no beneficial effects of this treatment." He agreed. The trial results were positive, and I had a head start on this benign treatment. It felt a little like Pascal's wager: if I took the drug and it was not effective, I had lost nothing. But if I had not taken it and it was effective, I would have lost valuable time. There is no way to be certain, although the study results suggest a more than minimal effect.

2. Getting the best treatment

A colleague of mine with long-standing type-1 diabetes, asked me one day about my relationship with my neurologist. His question was: "How long does your specialist spend with you during your regular visits?" I replied, "He doesn't get up from his seat until he is finished answering my last question. Why do you ask?" He replied: "Mine doesn't sit down, he's so eager to get onto the next patient." This vignette highlights the need for a therapy team in PD that is available, knowledgeable about PD and all its ramifications, and able to communicate effectively.

3. Yogi Berra said . . .

"When you reach a fork in the road, *take it*." Many such sayings have been attributed to Yogi, a Major League Baseball player with a penchant for battering the English language. I used this one in my retirement speech saying: "Parkinson was an uninvited interloper in our home. My family and I had reached a fork in the road we had been traveling. So, I took the left fork hoping that PD would "fork-off". But it was not to be. PD is like obnoxious boarders who play music too loud and leave a mess wherever they go.

4. "I sentence you to life."

PD is not so much a death sentence as it is a life sentence. I recently remarked to a colleague who has had PD for five years, that since my diagnosis, I haven't had a single good day. Oh, don't get me wrong, I have had, and continue to have, great days, just none when for twenty-four hours Parkinson does in fact "fork off." It is relentless.

One example of my good-great divide is that my insomnia was an opportunity in one way. Lying awake for hours on end caused considerable anxiety. My insomnia demanded that I fill the hours of wakefulness productively. So, over a three-year period I registered for the senior Doctor of Science in Medicine degree, the highest academic honour from my alma mater, the University of the Witwatersrand in Johannesburg, South Africa. Candidates for this degree compile the story of their research contributions, putting them in the context of the world literature. The document that I produced was carefully reviewed by international experts in the field, and the degree was awarded. It provided me with an excellent opportunity to reflect on the first thirty years of my career, as well as mitigate the angst, exhaustion and depression which comes from sleeplessness. But it did not "cure" the insomnia.

As physicians we often talk about Elizabeth Kubler-Ross's five stages of grief: denial, anger, pleading, depression, and finally acceptance. The five stages neither necessarily occur in all patients, nor in the same order. Nonetheless I found this an excellent model for my initial experience with PD. Most of the denial had subsided by the time the diagnosis was confirmed, the anger was more of a seething, and has, like the depression, never fully disappeared, surfacing from time to time. There was no bargaining, and acceptance is the reluctant submission to living the rest of one's life encumbered by the PD.

"DON'T YOU DARE CALL ME DISABLED OR COMMENT ON THE QUALITY OF MY LIFE."

Wallowing in despair is neither an emotion to which I commonly admit, nor one for which I need assistance. But the realities of PD have brought me close to it. Fending off these negative emotions takes a huge effort. Early in the course of my PD, I recall getting onto a full subway train, all seats were taken. A young woman recognizing my burden, kindly offered me her seat. I growled that I did not need to sit. I certainly wasn't going to admit that I needed a seat. Only afterwards did I recognize that this represented more than a little denial. The next offer of a seat was gracefully accepted.

I bristle at being called "disabled." It is such a minimizing/restricting word. I would much prefer "physically challenged" as describing the symptoms that evolve over time: more stiffness, body aches and pains, exhaustion. PD worsens with age and so do general health and well-being. As my mother used to say: "Ageing is not for sissies!" But it's all very well to dislike the impact of the PD, it is more important to learn to live with it.

FEAR

As the symptoms have progressed and I have gotten older, (I have no doubt that) it has caused me to become more fearful and timid, avoiding situations that previously I wouldn't have given two seconds' thought. An event that exemplified this occurred one evening when driving home from work. A young man stepped between two trucks and did not see me until his arm hit my passenger side mirror. Minor injury, his fault, but I stopped driving after that.

A major fear that develops with time is the fear of falling. This has made me ever more cautious. An enthusiast for travel, I have visited many places in Canada, the US, Europe, and Africa. Although still eager to go places, I have avoided remote locations— for example, I have always wanted to go to the Galapagos Islands. The thought of getting a complication of PD in so distant a place keeps me away. Nevertheless, since diagnosis I have been to many places for both academic and personal reasons, including: Lithuania to trace family roots; Normandy, France to visit the site of the D-Day landings in the Second World War; and game parks in South Africa, Botswana, and East Africa.

The COVID-19 pandemic has served to accentuate the concept of risk. The result is the shrinking of one's world.

PICTURE IMPERFECT

One of the most disconcerting things about PD is the distortions that are captured on camera. A hand in spasm, facial expressions (open mouthed gives a hang-dog look), and dyskinesias on home-made videos are just a few examples. This enhances the feeling of physical deterioration. Can mental deterioration be far behind? There are quite a few family photographs taken on holidays that epitomize this.

A ROYAL PAIN IN THE . . .

There are two features of PD that are increasingly troublesome. At the bottom end is the constipation. This a result of dysregulation of pelvic muscle function such that the stool hardens and becomes increasingly more difficult to expel. Dried peaches and apricots seem to do the trick for me.

At the top end, is that in some people with PD, the voice becomes softer and ever more difficult to hear. I do not perceive that anything is wrong with my voice, but my wife keeps reminding me to speak louder, and my friends and family keep asking me to repeat myself.

BIRDS OF A FEATHER DON'T STICK TOGETHER

While I have spoken to many people with PD themselves or with a family member with PD to help them find the best therapy or to counsel them at diagnosis, until recently I have studiously avoided being part of patient groups. Being in the company of someone with severe disease has always made me feel incredibly vulnerable, something that lasts well beyond the time of the meeting.

However, I recently joined a weekly physiotherapy group that meets for an hour of vigorous exercise every Friday afternoon. The exercises serve as the impetus for other activities through the rest of the week.

I also joined a support group that meets monthly for an afternoon of walking through different neighborhoods in town. Perhaps this means the support of the group is beginning to prove more beneficial than isolation.

FAMILY VALUES AND EXPECTATIONS

Having people in one's life who are understanding, supportive and loving helps ease the pain most of the time. I am indebted to my wife, sons and their families for their steadfast help in dealing with clinical ramifications in all aspects of PD. Some "fair-weather" friends might have flown the coop. More importantly, good friends remain.

I have adjusted slowly and carefully to the progression of PD: less flexible, more minor aches and pains and more awareness of so-called "off" times, when medications seem to wear off all at the same time. Also, awareness that "switch-on" is not instantaneous. It is difficult to explain these to someone who sees you as being the same.

LAYERING

I use this term, layering, to denote those times when PD and all its ramifications seem to be overwhelming. PD has had some significant behavioral effects which have waxed and waned over time. More irritable, less loquacious, and less adventurous, being wary (and weary) – all add up to being grumpier than before. When one adds other stressors to an already overloaded system, I would expect and have noticed my response being exaggerated.

An example: after about eight years with PD, my cell phone pinged at 5:30 one morning with a text message from my younger son, then thirty-eight and living in California: "If you are awake, call me," it said. When I called, he answered with: "Dad, I may have bladder cancer." It is more than eleven years later, and he has been cancer free since a tiny polyp was removed from his bladder. But getting through the early days after his diagnosis had two effects: it made me "forget" ("ignore" may be a better word) about the PD for a while, and to concentrate on his wellness. PD or no PD, this diagnosis in one's child is devastating. I still get very anxious at the time of his post-treatment screenings done annually. It a huge relief each year when he gets the "all clear" from his physicians.

Next came the pandemic. My older son is an infectious diseases physician in Toronto. I have taken his very strict safety precautions seriously. I worried (incessantly) about risks to our family members. Two years of my life have slipped by in the captivity of COVID-19 rules.

IT TAKES TWO TO TANGLE

In the summer of 2023, slap-bang in the middle of the pandemic, I had two falls. The first occurred while out walking the dog. I tripped on the curb and went flying forward onto my hands and knees. The result: a dislocated middle finger and two small fractures on my middle and index fingers, plus a scraped knee. I passed it off as a simple misstep, nothing really to be too concerned about. One episode doesn't necessarily portend future falls.

But, then a few weeks later, as I stood up quickly from a sitting position, I lurched forward hitting my head on a chair across the room. An ambulance was called, and I was taken to the nearest hospital, where a CT scan of my head was normal. The most positive result of this Emergency Room visit is that an Occupational Therapist was unleashed on my wife and me. She sorted out a walker for me, and expertly advised us on what home adjustments we needed to make our home safer, e.g. handrails inside and outside, making all carpets non-slip, and more.

These changes certainly have been helpful, and no further falls have occurred. They heavily underline the fact that there has been some important deterioration in my condition.

FINAL THOUGHTS

The description of my relationship to PD is complex and changing: do I control the PD, or does it control me? Has PD come to define me? I certainly hope not, but it does feel that way at times. I would like to think that the things that define who I am are more forgiving: father, husband, grandfather, physician, teacher, friend, mentor, to name just a few. But as PD becomes more externally noticeable—it is increasingly hard to mask its features—so I become more and more controlled by it, avoiding uncomfortable situations, such as standing around for any length of time (e.g. at receptions, queueing up for any reason, just chatting). Avoiding these stressors has the potential to isolate oneself either by choice or by impression. I retired from medical practice at age 67, largely because of the PD. I did not think it fair to my patients to continue. But I miss clinical medicine and its academic aspects (education and research) terribly. Nothing has been able to replace that loss. I read prolifically, exercise quite regularly, watch too many football and other sports teams, participate in discussions with a whole array of people and attend some medical rounds each week. A mere shadow of my former self.

And I continue my sentence, hoping it will last for some time yet.

"Life is not a matter of playing good cards, but of playing a bad hand well," said Robert Louis Stevenson.

PD is a lousy hand, but I think I've played it fairly well so far.

14

Living with Philosophical Isolation

AHMED

PHILOSOPHICAL ISOLATION MAY SOUND like an unusual adversity, but it is a struggle many confront. It arises from the loneliness of being an extreme minority in a sea of dogmatic ideas, and being denied all forms of self-expression.

"APOSTASY"

I believe in free speech, free thought, and secular humanism. As harmless as these beliefs might sound, I live in a country where they earn one a place among the enemy. Just the word "secularism" is inflammatory here, and my philosophical views especially warrant ostracism and government persecution. I lack religious faith in any personal god, from which follows a set of conclusions about the suffering of the world, the meaning of life, and whether I ought to have children. My "apostasy" alone is enough to warrant imprisonment; in countries that apply the Sharia law, it is even punishable by death.

Ironically, the cruelty of this law gives rise to the skepticism it attempts to suppress, and thus apostasy is born from the attempt to prevent it. In other words, one is killed for renouncing the evil in one's being killed.

The case of Sarah Hegazy comes to mind. She was a queer Egyptian who was arrested, imprisoned, and tortured for the "crime" of waving a rainbow flag at a concert. She was irreversibly traumatized and ultimately took her own life. Everyone who shares my views here is at risk of suffering her fate. There is zero tolerance for atheism, homosexuality, or any difference that challenges dogma.

I have friends from around the world—Lebanon, Morocco, and Pakistan—who are in the same danger. That danger is why you would never find an "apostate" publicly "come out" here. It is not only because they are an extreme statistical minority. You might pass them on the street, but just like me, they will hide their thoughts. You would never guess mine if you met me; I have mastered the art of putting on that show.

Over time, one internalizes the judgments this elaborate performance protects one from; an inner critic scrutinizes one's intelligence, education, intellectual honesty, and even morals. It is only natural that one develops such a harsh inner voice, when one has grown into the person one's child-self was indoctrinated to hate the most.

However, while my views fall under the umbrella of "philosophical pessimism," they do not entail any of the immorality, nihilism, misanthropy, hopelessness, or despair I was raised to associate them with. I simply find it impossible to *convince myself* of otherworldly claims, or that all the world's suffering happens under the supervision of an all-loving, all-powerful god. Neither can I accept any justification for "eternal damnation."

I sincerely cannot help but reject that which my mind recognizes as false, cruel, and sadistic, but this alone deems one "willfully deaf, dumb, and blind" (Qur'an 2:18) if one is born in the wrong place.

FAMILIAL ISOLATION

I choose to hide my thoughts for reasons beyond the fear of government persecution. I also do so for the sake of those I love, who would see my renunciation of religious faith as a vile crime, tantamount to murder. They freely condemn disbelievers in small talk, because they cannot fathom that those whom they demonize are not "westerners" thousands of miles away, but right within earshot. Never can they imagine that I, the "good" person they admire and love, could write this. Ironically, their good image of me is not necessarily a façade, because all they see—my behavior, personality, lifestyle, and treatment of others—is all there is.

Apart from my thoughts, nothing is hidden; I am not leading some depraved double life. Thus, one could argue that my loved ones' good perception of me is not undeserved, but they would instantly see me as a devil and "infidel" if my true beliefs were to be known. I often catch a glimpse of that dreaded possibility, when I am told, directly after being praised, "*But what about consistent prayer, Ahmed? I feel guilty thinking your negligence as a Muslim is my fault.*"

The sudden shift from affection to guilt makes it clear that religion always comes first. Dogma subconsciously qualifies affection; it poisons the sincerest sentiments, tears apart even the strongest bonds, and denies one the only family one will ever have.

I could only imagine the catastrophe if it were discovered that I am not even a "negligent" Muslim, but not a Muslim at all. Thus, I export to the outside world an external shell of who I am, and I maintain two identities: one engages in peaceful, non-confrontational talk with family and everyone else, and the other is writing this. The second identity is the most fragile part of myself: it is vulnerable to attacks of shame, hatred, and even physical harm. Thus, I shield it with the first. With that shield up, I feel stable, safe, and protected.

It is not an exaggeration to say that the fabric of my reality is a web of lies and deceit. Without the shield, when my tongue slips or the terrifying prospect of being "outed" seems too imminent, that "stability" of my world crumbles. I feel unclothed. My chest tightens with intense fear and shame, as if all eyes are upon my exposed, vulnerable body. The urge to disappear quickly takes over me, and I suddenly find safety in hiding behind the isolation that brings me suffering.

I live knowing that a genuine part of me evokes disgust; that it ought to be hidden and *protected* from the hatred of even my loved ones, till either my death or theirs. The thought of their death is especially painful: to think that death will, first, pitilessly annihilate one's loved ones; then deliver the final blow, by cementing one's lie as eternal. In other words, even after death, they will never come to know my true self.

Still, I deem it the lesser of two evils, for the alternative of losing and hurting those I care about feels nothing short of apocalyptic. I go to great lengths to avoid that chaotic doomsday: I hide all digital instances of what I write, read, and think that can be traced back to me; I even take part in rituals I have no faith in. In an odd way, such rituals bring me comfort—no thanks to a long-gone spirituality, but because performing them publicly reinforces the illusion of conformity behind which I hide. The *deliberate* effort of doing so restores a calming sense of control.

Every year, I present the façade of "fasting" during Ramadan, and I abstain from food from sunrise to sunset, occasionally drinking water in secret. I remember how this secrecy used to fill me with near-constant anxiety. Every thought carried the guilt of a felony, and every action the fear of being "caught." One indeed feels like a felon taking a sip of water in the daylight of Ramadan, when one resorts to clandestine means to commit a criminalized—yet trivial—act.

Luckily, time desensitizes one; the anxiety lessens as living in secrecy becomes second nature, but it never goes away. Rationally, I recognize that nothing about my views remotely warrants hatred; that I ought not to seek the acceptance of those who would *unfairly* reject me. However, one cannot, in good conscience, dismiss one's loved ones as irrelevant enemies when they have always treated one in ways an enemy never would. Nor can one dismiss the valid rationale behind one's "heretical" views. From that dissonance emerges loneliness.

One is admired yet feels like an outsider, a *fraud*, because of the realization that only the partial identity one presents earns conditional affection. That which is buried underneath is one slip-of-the-tongue away from rendering one irreversibly unacceptable and unlovable.

I have many times considered the possibility that I might be mistaken in my beliefs, hence worthy of loneliness, hatred, and suffering. I do so every day. Perhaps one day, through some miracle or an act of divine intervention, all the reasons I have accumulated throughout the years in favor of my views would be countered. I am open to the possibility that one book, or one random thought, could be all it takes to override everything I know.

However, I would still not understand why, in that fateful moment, this single burst of newfound faith would magically transform me from a lost "soul" to one that has found salvation. The implication of accepting this is that the thoughtcrime of skepticism nullifies a good life. That implication is widely accepted in my country; the consensus is that "shirk" (Arabic for disbelief or polytheism) is the only unforgivable sin. That sin is said to be punishable by an eternity of torture in "fire fueled with people and stones" (Qur'an 2:24), but other than that, the gates of heaven are so wide that even a mass murderer could waltz right in!

Such vain threats of eternal punishment, and the death penalty for apostasy mentioned earlier, share the same self-defeating irony: the "punishment" arouses the very skepticism it punishes. Valid ideas welcome criticism; none but false, fragile ideologies subdue it. That irony also carries a potent, reassuring argument: one could not be wrong in one's disbelief in a "benevolent" God, who would (infinitely) torment one for being "wrong."

ON NOT PUNCTURING DELUSIONS

I have always heard my family say "Alhamdulillah," Arabic for "thanks be to Allah/God." Through financial troubles, my father's cancer diagnosis, chemotherapy treatment, and all other hardships, they drew comfort from their faith in God's benevolent plan. I think none of it follows any divine plan, but I feel no urge to tell them that they construct their entire existence on a delusion.

Nor do I feel inclined to tell my mother that my father's cancer was a byproduct of blind, utterly indifferent forces; that there is no afterlife, no compensation for the pointless suffering his illness caused him, and that we will not see him—or, after our own deaths, each other—ever again. I have no desire to tell her that if the god to whom she is thankful exists, then an attitude of gratitude is deeply misguided. There is no reason to add the pain of existential angst to an already long list of suffering. I fear causing another sort of pain, of which I saw a glimpse when, in a conversation with my older sister, the afterlife came up.

Without a hint of doubt or skepticism in her eyes, she said, "One must accept within his heart that *all* good moral deeds are irrelevant if not done for the sake of the 'right' creator. Only then will one be saved from eternal hellfire."

I was shocked to witness an intelligent, educated, and empathetic mind expressing unjustifiable prejudice against billions—the overwhelming majority of humans to have ever existed, including *me*, unbeknownst to her. Witnessing your sibling defend, with great fervor, the viewpoint that you should be tormented for all eternity is strangely absurd. Naturally, I felt the urge to object, but there was nothing else I could have done but nod and smile.

One must ask: what would happen if the target of this prejudice became *concrete*, and no longer an abstract artifact from a distant society? When it becomes *me*, someone she is familiar with, loves, and thinks highly of, would that nudge her unshakable faith? I did not seek to uncover the answer to that question. Doing so would have cost me a great deal (her love and acceptance), but it also would have brought her pain—internal conflict, shock, disillusionment, and grief.

To her, it would not be as if the person she had always known changed beyond recognition, but rather that he died; she would dread the fate she thinks awaits him in the "afterlife." Even my father, who was a strong believer, is a subject of such dread and grief simply because he neglected one core pillar of Islam—prayer. I comfort my mother saying he will be okay, for Allah is all-merciful. When it comes to my fate, however, the limits of His mercy are crystal clear (at least in any honest interpretation), and there would be no comforting lie she could reluctantly accept. I would rather avoid adding to her pain.

Such pain could, in principle, lead to understanding and acceptance. However, considering the regrettable state of education and intellectual discourse in my country, culture, and immediate environment, such a beneficial result is unlikely in practice. One cannot attain a different perspective or entertain a different idea when there is only a single idea in the "marketplace" of ideas. They will not accept my worldview, nor accept me for having it.

I have grappled with the possibility that my reasoning may reveal a deeply buried narcissism or sense of intellectual superiority. I was disturbed to consider whether my concealment of the truth suggests an elitist attitude, but I would argue that I am employing common sense and empathy. I believe the moral choice is to keep to myself, to avoid guilt and lessen the suffering that, in my case and for the reasons I have shown, I consider of no instrumental value.

TO BLAME OR NOT TO BLAME?

In my early stages of deconversion a few years ago, I experienced a lot of anger. Anger at the intense state of loneliness, the stifling ignorance and religious intolerance that plagues this country, the lack of empathy, the suffering and injustice of the world, and the countless moral atrocities committed in the name of God. The major shift in worldview and identity also carried its challenges. Making like-minded friends over the internet has helped, and I am grateful one of them is nearby and has been my friend in real life for a few years.

Over time, I have learned to cope with and mitigate some of my anger, through seeing my situation as a consequence of a random and indifferent universe in which everyone is a victim. This might sound strange to some, but I find it difficult to blame anybody entirely for their childhood indoctrination, ignorance, lack of education, or their inability to change the subjective perspective that defines their entire reality.

Intelligent and moral people can believe in silly things that divide them, and I do not think it is necessarily a choice. I find anger and hatred to be exhausting, and empathy to be a healthy substitute. This approach has allowed my love for my family to survive the forces of ignorance and dogma unscathed, through extending the acceptance I know will not be reciprocated. Thus, I do not argue against their prejudice because there is nothing to gain, and everything to lose, from engaging in this foolish attempt.

I do not need them to share my views, nor do I need them even to accept the real me, because while they would attempt to convert me so they could allow themselves to love me again, I do not require such a condition. I can see past their beliefs and acknowledge they are great people worth loving—a courtesy they would not grant me.

RELATIONAL ISOLATION

Dogma has the potential to undermine friendship, when some secrets can never be shared with even the closest friend. I have grown emotionally distant from my childhood friend because of his incessant intolerant remarks that he cannot fathom apply to me. Though I do not blame him (for the reasons I stated), I cannot help but feel distant.

It also can preclude any possibility of "romantic" relationships. For one who wishes to remain permanently child-free and could only be accepted by a secular partner, the pool of possible partners is only a miniscule proportion of my country's population. The prospect of relationships is, to put it mildly, statistically unlikely. Thus, when I imagine the future, I do not envision a lifelong partner or family.

My isolation currently manifests in the concealment of my true self from my loved ones, but after they have gone, I envision it as physical. I am not in despair over this future, nor do I seek to prevent it, as I seem to have gradually accepted it as realistically unavoidable.

My attitude towards "romance" is analogous to how one does not despair or dwell on the odds of winning the lottery; if it miraculously happens, one would be delighted, but if it does not, one is indifferent.

My family often wholesomely brings up marriage, to which I internally let out an ironic laugh and jokingly reply: "I don't think you understand that you're stuck with me. There's no getting rid of me that easily!"

Dogma can also manifest in controlling and abusive families. Even if one is lucky enough to find a compatible partner, one's family and society might disapprove. One could even be forced into living with a partner one did not choose—an appalling fate worse than loneliness.

Intuitively, escaping to a better country is the optimal solution. Elsewhere, one would find the intellectual compatibility and acceptance one desires. One's autonomy would not be violated, and perhaps the prospect of romantic relationships, in that case, would not seem so outlandish.

However, in my specific case, I am not entirely certain. On the one hand, it seems that I would not fully let go of my native tongue, culture, childhood foods, home, and family whom I deeply love. I am not sure I ought to let go; not even sure I want to. On the other, my inner world has lost its sense of harmonious "belonging" that once accompanied shared belief—alongside all blissful childhood delusions.

Growing up has changed not only my beliefs but also my consciousness. Hence, one could ask: is it worth the hassle of being estranged in a foreign country for the sake of acceptance and possibly romantic "love," if the price is leaving behind everything one would miss?

For many in my situation, the *objective* answer is an emphatic "yes." My answer is ambivalent, as it seems I am caught between cultures, and I fully belong to neither. My place of birth, with which I am familiar, utterly rejects me, but foreign lands are blocked by a mountain of immigration laws that I am not sure is worth climbing.

FINAL WORDS

I have maintained that an attitude of empathy is preferable to anger. However, one must acknowledge it is difficult to forgive those who abuse and control one, or those who violate one's bodily autonomy or lifestyle. Thus, a different attitude would be appropriate for a woman in Afghanistan or Iran (or even here in Egypt) who is forced into a burqa and an arranged marriage, or sentenced to death for exercising basic human rights. This happens every day, and none of it is forgivable.[1]

---

1. I dedicate this essay to my family, whom I know will never read this but whom I love, and to my friends, whose acceptance palliates my isolation.

15

Living with Psychosis

Abigail Gosselin

In summer 2017, while at a conference in Seattle, I suffered a psychotic break. An invisible force was pulling me toward the water, and every chance I got, I had to walk the mile from the university where I was staying down to the docks. I paced along the pier for what seemed like hours, and then I trudged back to campus to try to participate in the conference as best as I could. While I walked, pieces of me dripped off until there was nothing left of me, no "I" to hold everything together. In the conference I was vacant and disturbed, feeling that pull toward the water. Feeling sub-human, I could not talk to anyone except a friend who accompanied me to the conference, and I had trouble making eye contact or smiling. Without an "I" to hold everything together, there was no basis for human contact, and a chasm separated the bits of me that remained from the world around me, including other people. Another night in Seattle, and I would have spent the night pacing the docks, muttering to myself.

I have had bipolar disorder for most of my adult life, but this was the first time I experienced an episode of psychosis without an accompanying mood change. Although I made it home from the conference safely, the psychosis remained as I started the fall semester of teaching. Without a context for understanding what I was going through, I felt confused and disoriented and tried my best to hold it together so I could do my job as a professor and take care of my family. For the duration of the fall semester, I struggled to participate in the reality that everyone else inhabits, feeling pulled by an invisible force into a separate world inside my head.

This world captivated me with its strange sensations and feelings of special meaning permeating certain things. Certain songs I listened to told me what to feel and what to think, and kept my mind locked in a constant album track while the record player played that same groove over and over again. Some objects became infused with meaning, as something random suddenly became something special, and I harped on this specialness, trying to figure out what message it was trying to send me. Most compelling of all was the quality of the sunlight: the angle and brightness of the sun rays often felt creepy to me, making me feel as if I were in a waking nightmare. Sometimes the angle and brightness of the sun made me feel welcome and hopeful, but often it pressed down upon me like something terrible was about to happen. Yet even as the sun made me so uneasy, I felt compelled to be outside in it as much as possible, soaking up the feelings it was transmitting to me.

Psychosis greatly diminished my comprehension. Incessant noise in my head was so loud it often drowned out other sounds in the world outside my head, to the point where I often could not hear, never mind understand, other people when they talked to me. I could not see the larger context that gives discrete events or objects meaning, so events and objects felt random and disconnected to me. This made reading nearly impossible; the best I could do was skip around a page and try to fill in the pieces in between, to try to make sense of the random bits of words I could see. Being unable to follow plot lines in movies, I watched movies without understanding what was happening, just absorbing flashes of dialogue and action without anything to hold it together. When looking at handouts in faculty meetings, I could not recognize that the handout in front of me was the same one that had been emailed to me. It was processed in a different moment in time and thus appeared to me to be entirely different.

Being caught up in the world inside my head, preoccupied with the constant noise in my head and the strange sensations I was experiencing, made interacting with other people extremely difficult. It was so hard to hear people, to process what they were saying, and to think of something to say in response. Consequently, I stopped talking to people as much as possible. When it was unavoidable, as in the classroom, I relied on stock exchanges and habitual responses. I had taught my classes so many times at that point that I knew what would come up in conversation, and I knew how to respond to it to move discussion along. As much as possible, I avoided situations where I would have to talk with someone one-on-one, because it was too hard to process a conversation that intense and too much pressure to have to say something intelligent in response. When I did have one-on-one conversations, I relied on stock responses such as saying, "Yeah," to sound like I was tracking the conversation even though I wasn't. Most conversations with me were one-sided as I tried to trick the person I was talking to into believing I was following along even though I could hardly hear or understand what they were saying.

These aspects of psychosis crept up on me over the course of the fall semester, until the winter when I was utterly in its grasp. By then, I was hearing a voice telling me to kill myself, and my brain was in a constant fog of disorganization, confusion, and disorientation. Feeling despondent over my inability to understand the world around me, I became depressed and suicidal and took seriously the voice I heard. Everything continued to get worse until I walked into a crisis center in April 2018 and asked to be hospitalized. I was put on a seventy-two-hour mental health hold, and placed in a psychiatric hospital, where I stayed for a week. Antipsychotic medication helped alleviate the psychosis, but even when that was under control, the suicidality came roaring back.

For months after being released from the hospital, I wavered between psychosis and suicidality; when one was under control (largely due to medication), the other flared up. I felt trapped in my illness, like I would always be sick, and I came to see myself as essentially a sick person. In the spring and fall of 2018, I spent months in the behavioral health clinic's intensive outpatient program (IOP), attending three-hour sessions three times a week, squeezing them in between my classes. Half of an IOP session was a class where we learned techniques for distress tolerance and mindfulness, and half was group therapy where we shared how we were doing. Gradually, over the course of these months, I began to see myself as more than a sick person, as someone capable of coping. I learned techniques that I was able to put into practice, and this helped me feel like I had more control over my situation, making me feel less despondent. Partly because of IOP and partly because of changes in medication, the depression lifted. However, in January 2019, the psychosis returned, and again I retreated into a world inside my mind.

The voice in my head constantly told me what to do. Mostly it told me to do things I was going to do anyway, but sometimes it told me to use my time differently, such as to go hiking instead of reading philosophy. I felt compelled to do what it told me to do; I did not know the consequences of disobeying, but I did not want to find out. The "I" that normally holds everything together became unraveled again, and I sent my therapist and psychiatrist crazed, rambling emails that seemed to me to be about something important but really were about nothing. I went back to avoiding people as much as possible and became enamored with strange sensations, such as a sensation in my nose (not a smell) that told me how to feel, and I became obsessed with finding hidden meanings in song lyrics and in random objects like garbage lying on the side of the road. My comprehension again plummeted, and teaching became continuously harder.

One of the worst effects of psychosis for me was the way it seemed to have an agency of its own that tried to supersede my own will and agency. In telling me what to do, how to feel, and what to think, it took over my mind as its ruler, and it controlled my mental states and behavior. Early in the psychosis, I was confused about this and didn't understand what was ruling over me; I just knew that I wasn't in charge of myself anymore. I identified it as an invisible force, or what I came to call "the voice," but I did not understand where it came from. The longer I was psychotic, the more I became aware that it was my psychosis that was trying to rule me, that the voice I heard and the pull I felt came directly from it. This understanding did not diminish the force of the psychosis in any way; it just allowed me to personify the psychosis as "the voice," an entity with its own will that wanted to rule over my will and supersede my agency with its own agency. My struggle against psychosis was a struggle against a personified force that I knew was at root illness, yet that remained powerful even with that awareness.

One of the most significant aspects of my psychosis's will was its desire to perpetuate itself. It often told me to reduce or stop my anti-psychotic medication so that it could rear its face more strongly than ever. Reducing my anti-psychotic medication was in fact often a trigger for increased psychosis. The psychosis told me to perform actions that kept me within its grasp and made it harder to heal and harder to function. It made me withdraw from other people, keeping me socially isolated, and prevented me from doing all the tasks that were expected of me at work and home. The psychosis wanted to keep me inside the world in my mind, untethered to the reality outside of my head, always floating above it, unable to perceive it or interact with it properly.

In disorganizing my mind and reducing my comprehension and understanding, psychosis diminished my competence, my self-confidence, my self-trust, my self-esteem, my sense of myself as an agent, and ultimately my understanding of my personal identity. Feeling like I was constantly in a brain fog where even ordinary things often did not make sense to me, I struggled to feel like I was good at anything. Certainly I felt incompetent as a teacher, writer, and colleague (hence as a professor), and also as a mother, wife, and daughter. Because I felt like I could not fulfill the expectations associated with my various roles, I felt like a failure. I could not trust myself to be able to adequately perform many tasks that I used to be able to do, and I did not trust myself to be able to figure out what to say or how to react when people spoke to me or otherwise interacted with me. My confidence plummeted, and I felt very hesitant and unsure about doing any tasks, especially those involved with interacting with people. I thought very poorly of myself and believed I lost my ability to be an agent as well as lost the identity I formerly had.

With my diminished competence, agency, self-confidence, self-trust, and self-esteem, I became very dependent on my husband. Not trusting myself to understand what situation I found myself, or to figure out how to respond to my situation adequately, I leaned on him to do the understanding and responding for me. I let him do all the talking, all the dealing with people, all the social interaction. At most, I just tried to listen alongside him, trying to make sense of what was going on around me. My ability to solve problems and cope with difficulties plummeted, and I relied on him to do the necessary problem-solving and dealing with various issues. While I could do things that were in my normal, everyday routine, because I knew how to go through the motions even if I could not be fully present, I could not do anything outside of that routine.

My dependency on my husband, as well as my need for him to be a caretaker to me, transformed our relationship in a very negative way. When he had to take on the responsibility of suicide-proofing the house by hiding kitchen knives and such, he balked. He did it because he had to, but he hated it. When I wasn't in control of my own safety, he had the burden of taking on that responsibility, a responsibility that was just too great for a person to bear when they are supposed to be an equal partner. It transformed him into my caretaker, a role he did not want—not because he didn't want to take care of me, but because he wanted me to be an equal partner to him. He wanted us to be *interdependent*, caring for each other; but, unable to care for myself properly, I was equally unable to care for him, so all the care work fell on him alone. This was unfair to him and detrimental to our relationship.

As I got better, and safety was less of an issue, I gradually relearned how to take care of myself, and I gradually developed the capacity to care for him as well. When we were able to be more equal in the relationship, we were able to repair our relationship, and it probably became stronger as a result of working through such trials. My commitment to him strengthened, as did my resolve to be the best person I could be, so that I could be there for him—and for our children. He and they provided me with significant motivation to learn how to take care of myself, which gave me the ability in turn to take care of them.

Recovery was still miles away when, in June 2019, I again filled with despair and became suicidal, feeling incapable of ever getting better. By this time, my mind was so sick I knew that I was incapable of doing my job and feared I would have to go on short-term disability when the fall semester started. In lieu of hospitalization or a suicide attempt, I returned to IOP, trying to soak in the skills I had been taught before. I also added a second antipsychotic medication to my regimen, risperidone. Taking risperidone was like turning on a light switch. Immediately the disorganization in my mind straightened out, and I was able to think more clearly. At first the change was subtle, but it was definitely there.

Over the next several weeks, my mind cleared considerably. The noise in my head quieted down, and the strange sensations dissipated. I saw that there was nothing behind what had seemed like hidden meanings, no secret messages to decode or transmit. Reading became easier, plot lines became understandable, and conversations made sense. Able now to hear and understand what people were saying, I could even think of things to say in response. By the time the fall semester started in August, I was capable of interacting with people and doing my job. I did not need to consider disability anymore. Instead, I just had to learn to live with taking all this antipsychotic medication.

Antipsychotic medication can be hard to get used to. My first medication, ziprasidone, gave me a constant tremor and made me shake visibly and uncontrollably when I was nervous. It made me very tired, and I had to experiment with how to take it so it would not sedate me. Risperidone was even more sedating. If I don't set an alarm clock, I easily sleep for ten or eleven hours on risperidone. So, I set an alarm clock every day, even on weekends. I have always been a runner, and for the first couple of months of taking risperidone, I would feel wiped out for a full morning after even a short run. Gradually exertion became easier, and my energy levels stabilized so that months later I could feel normal during and after a run and have a normal amount of energy to get through the day. Thankfully these medications did not affect my appetite or weight.

For me, psychosis was episodic, not constant. In the throes of psychosis, I felt like it had always been there and always would be there, but that is not how it really was. I became psychotic in response to a stressful period of traveling, after months of workplace stress that I did not know how to deal with. When I was in depressed and manic episodes, I experienced aspects of psychosis, but they faded when my moods stabilized. This was the first time I had experienced psychosis without a corresponding mood change, and it seemed to me as if my bipolar disorder had turned into schizoaffective disorder. Before this period of psychosis, I often experienced intense feelings and intense reactions to events; while I was psychotic, I felt nothing at all. Affectless, I felt no emotion and was unable to express emotion either verbally or though body language, unable to laugh or cry, unable even to smile. My mood disorder seemed to turn into a thought disorder. Even now that my psychosis has been abated for a few years, I still do not feel anything intensely—though I am able to laugh, smile, and otherwise show emotion. I am not sure if I even have bipolar disorder anymore, but I know that psychosis is always a threat on the horizon if I don't take care of myself and don't take my medication as prescribed.

In response to the neurodiversity movement, the anti-psychiatry movement, and aspects of the peer support movement which claim that psychosis is a mere difference that must be tolerated, not a pathology that must be treated, I argue that psychosis often creates objective harms that make a person's life much more difficult, more isolated, more disabled, and more despairing. Not being able to connect to reality in the right way makes it very difficult to interact appropriately with others and very difficult to take care of oneself. It is not only a person's social relationships that are harmed, but also the core of being human: their agency and autonomy are diminished, and their personal identity is changed for the worse. That is not to say that psychosis is *only* bad; a person can find some good in their psychotic experience as well. But the bad effects of psychosis often harm a person deeply and make their life worse. Treating psychosis through psychological and medical means such as therapy and medication is essential.

Because my mental health crises have always been episodic, I know that even though I feel healed currently, there is a good chance I will experience another psychotic episode in the future, and possibly a mood episode may return as well. However, I am taking medication that I have never taken before this period (both the antipsychotic medications, and anti-depressants and anti-anxiety medications that even out my mood), and these may buffer or even prevent any future psychotic or mood episode I may face. So, I do not feel hopeless against my mental illness, just vigilant, always aware that it could spring up again. However, with the tools I learned in my last mental health crisis (especially distress tolerance, mindfulness, and gentleness with myself), and the medications I am now on, I know that I will probably be able to cope better if I do get sick again. In contrast to how I felt when I was sick, I am now hopeful for the future and more confident in my ability to cope with stress, adversity, and psychosis, and in my ability to heal and recover from a mental health episode. Living with psychosis has been very challenging, but I have found ways to cope and heal.

16

Living with Public Shame

Rebecca Tuvel

SHAME IS A FUNNY thing. It doesn't answer to reason. It resists the passage of time. Shame engulfs the self. You didn't just *do* a bad thing. You *are* a bad person.

In 2017, I found myself at the center of a notorious online shaming in academia. I now regard my experience as the target of a massive online pile-on as one of the best things that ever happened to me. Yet it was also one of the worst. Writing about it is hard. At the time, I was an assistant professor of philosophy at Rhodes College, where I remain today. I have since been promoted to associate professor and department chair. I imagine my critic's voice: "Here goes Tuvel complaining about being a 'victim' of online shaming. She reeks of privilege." Another: "Tuvel wrote a terrible article that shouldn't have been published and should've cost her her job. But instead, her article got tons of citations, and she now has a cushy tenured position. Please throw her a pity party!"

Shh. Ignore the voices. No guilt, no holding back.

THE BACKLASH

My transgression? A piece I published in *Hypatia*, a top journal in feminist philosophy. My article, "In Defense of Transracialism," explores the wildly divergent reactions people have to transgender people on the one hand, and transracial people on the other. I argue that the considerations supporting acceptance of transgender individuals (those who seek to change sex) also support accepting *transracial* individuals (those who seek to change race). The contrast between reactions to transgender and transracial people was on stark display in June 2015. That month, *Vanity Fair* featured a photograph of transgender woman Caitlyn Jenner on the cover of their upcoming issue with the caption "Call me Caitlyn." Less than two weeks later, former NAACP chapter head Rachel Dolezal, who identified as black, was revealed to have white parents.

The media juxtaposition between Jenner and Dolezal sparked a series of challenging philosophical questions. What makes one kind of trans identity legitimate but not another kind of trans identity? What *are* sex, gender, and race? And can they be changed? If transgender people should be permitted to change their legal sex category, should transracial people be permitted to change their legal race category? Philosophers had written little on this last question. So, I set out to defend the argument that transgender acceptance implies transracial acceptance.

My article was online for about a month in 2017 before the backlash began. I first learned a controversy was brewing when someone with whom I went to graduate school emailed me to tell me that people on social media were coordinating a response to my article. People were especially upset by my use of the term "transgenderism," which they considered pathologizing. They also complained that I "deadnamed" Caitlyn Jenner. You deadname a trans person when you refer to them by a name they formerly used, such as their birth name. My stomach sank as I stood motionless in a store parking lot. It was the first sign of a gathering storm.

Two days later, an official "Open Letter to *Hypatia*" was widely circulated online. The letter called for my article to be retracted on the grounds that its "continued availability causes further harm." My article's supposed failings included that it (1) employed vocabulary and frameworks "not recognized, accepted, or adopted by the conventions of the relevant subfields" (e.g. used the term "transgenderism"), engaged in "deadnaming a trans woman"; (2) mischaracterized "theories and practices relating to religious identity and conversion" (e.g., gave an "off-hand example about conversion to Judaism"); (3) misrepresented "leading accounts of belonging to a racial group" (e.g. "incorrectly cite[d] Charles Mills as a defender of voluntary racial identification"); and (4) failed to "seek out and sufficiently engage with scholarly work by those who are most vulnerable to the intersection of racial and gender oppressions (women of color)."

Over 800 people signed the letter, including prominent feminist and trans thinkers. In response to the open letter, a majority of *Hypatia*'s associate editors issued a "profound apology" for the "harms that the publication on transracialism has caused," without the journal's Chief Editor's approval. A feminist philosopher whose argument in defense of a disanalogy between transgender and transracial identity I had critiqued in my article, publicly posted the apology on Facebook.

Meanwhile, on social media, feminist colleagues started to attack me personally. They called me "stupid," "ignorant," "racist," "transphobic," a "TERF" (a trans-exclusionary radical feminist), a "disgusting person," and a "nobody." In a popular Facebook post, one feminist accused me of enacting "violence" and perpetuating "harm." I was repeatedly called a "Becky" and "Rebecky Tuvel." "Becky" is a gendered and racialized insult that refers to a 'basic' stereotypical cis-gendered white woman; it's not a term you'd expect fellow feminists to use. Some people sent hate mail. The second email I received about the controversy had the subject line "Fuck you." Others called for me to be fired. At least one person threatened to contact the members of my tenure committee. Former feminist mentors publicly denounced me and privately tried to persuade me to retract my article.

One feminist philosopher, who was my undergraduate thesis advisor and a mentor I deeply respected, publicly posted: "I believe Rebecca wrote from a desire to do anti-oppressive work. I don't think she succeeded. I hope for her sake and for that of others that she will voluntarily retract the article and I have told her this."

Another feminist philosopher, whom I shall call Professor Gray, and who was a member of my dissertation committee, publicly condemned my article and called me to persuade me to retract my article voluntarily. She said that from her perspective, the "thing to do would be to apologize and retract the paper" and to abandon my book project since it "would be a career destroyer." She reassured me, though, that she was "not going to sabotage me or something like that." Our phone call ended with her telling me that I appeared incapable of giving a "sufficiently self-critical response" to the situation.

Professor Gray later reported she felt pressure from graduate students to "do something" about my article. I have no doubt. I witnessed the enormous pressure many philosophers exerted on others to denounce me publicly. It was a test. If you failed, you were a stupid racist transphobe just like Tuvel! A feminist who works in trans theory dared to voice a dissenting opinion on Facebook at one point. She was told to "fuck off" and that "trans folx can't trust her anymore."

I'll pause here to address a question people often ask: Didn't I *know* my article would invite a huge backlash? In short, no; It's nearly impossible to predict what will and or won't cause a social media shitstorm; there are just too many unpredictable factors. Of course, I *knew* my article presented a controversial argument on a sensitive topic, so I *did* expect that some people might read it, strongly disagree, and perhaps even respond. But that's the most I thought would happen.

After all, I did my due diligence. I solicited feedback and presented the paper multiple times, including to around thirty philosophers at our field's most competitive conference, the Eastern American Philosophical Association. And I submitted my paper specifically to *Hypatia* so that experts in feminist and trans philosophy could review it. Contrary to rumors circulating online, not one piece of feedback I received on the paper was out of the ordinary in philosophy. Not a peep about the ostensibly problematic terms I used or the offensiveness of writing the paper as a "cisgender white woman," which I believe was the biggest concern. Sure, some folks who raised objections appeared displeased. But that's par for the course in philosophy.

I learned much later that the *Hypatia* affair began with a Facebook post from a then-graduate student in Sociology, who condemned *Hypatia* for publishing what she called an "absolutely disgusting and harmful legitimization of 'transracial' identity . . ." She then solicited help drafting an open letter to the journal to ensure "this garbage [does not] gain traction." Notably, she ended her post with a request for someone to send her a copy of my paywalled article so she could "read it and properly put forth a response." The student hadn't even read my paper. She based her post entirely on the abstract of my paper.

PERSONAL IMPACT

I'll say this: I never could have predicted my reaction to being publicly shamed. I didn't sleep or eat for four days straight. I was glued to the computer. I became hugely paranoid that someone would dredge up material to use to attack me with online. To prevent further backlash, I withdrew a chapter I wrote on ecofeminism that was slated to appear in *The Edinburgh Companion to Animal Studies*. I obsessively read everything about the controversy I could find—all in a futile effort to gain some semblance of control. I swung wildly between fits of despair and elation. I burst into the bedroom at 4 a.m. one night, overjoyed to tell my partner about some article I had come across that took a sympathetic stance on transracialism. It wasn't until he told me my behavior was scaring him that I made an appointment to see a psychologist, who said I had experienced a hypomanic episode in response to the event.

Looking back, Gray was right about one thing: I probably *couldn't* provide a "sufficiently self-critical response" at the time. I doubt many people can. Shame threatens to dissolve the self, and self-criticism requires a self to criticize. Unlike guilt, which attaches to a specific act, shame ensnares your entire person before ejecting you from the moral community. Shame's defeat is totalizing. Unforgiving. As Gray herself writes in an essay of hers: "The burning feeling of shame, the sense of being out of place, judged by others as unworthy, unwanted, or wrong—not only in this particular action but in one's very existence—leaves the shameful subject nowhere to be, and yet nowhere to hide or escape."

The shameful person is toxic and contagious—get too close, and we may need to quarantine you. In fact, the initial source of impurity in the transracialism controversy wasn't me, but Dolezal herself, whose reputation had been tarnished two years earlier. I allowed Dolezal's toxicity to contaminate me by taking a sympathetic stance on the idea of transracialism. And anyone who wanted to sympathize with me, in turn, also risked tarnishing their reputation. The message to my potential supporters was clear: Feel badly for Tuvel? Send her a private email. Want to respond to her argument in writing? Do it without citing her directly. Want to condemn publicly how she's been treated? All right but clarify that you *disagree* with her argument and that her article had *lots* of problems.

I suspect that the desire to gain distance from the shameful person explains the rumor that I'd been "told" my paper was "problematic" but simply ignored the advice. Only that would vindicate the (at least) three philosophers (two of whom were friendly acquaintances) who attended my talk at the big conference, said not one word to me about my paper's supposed harms, and signed either the open letter or apology denouncing my paper. Two of those philosophers are people I had spent time with on several occasions.

The third philosopher, whom I shall call Professor Lane, was an editor at *Hypatia*. Lane added her name to the "profound apology" issued by the associate editors. How could Lane responsibly condemn my article on social media and sign an apology after passing up an opportunity to share her concerns with me in person? As it happened, Lane posed only one question during my talk, entirely unrelated to the issues that later caused outrage.

But the worst effects of public shaming, for me, were epistemic—that is, related to knowledge. Your sense of reality gets distorted. You want to hear and process the objections, but it's nearly impossible when people keep attacking your character. You get defensive, and this threatens your ability to think clearly.

"Am I a horrible person? A racist transphobe who wrote an unforgivably bad and dangerous article?" "Is my paper's argument so awful that I should retract it? So far, no one calling for my article's retraction has raised a compelling objection to the argument itself. But what if I'm missing something? I always say that humility is the philosopher's first virtue. Am I being sufficiently humble?"

Even though in her book, Caitlyn Jenner refers to herself when she was Bruce, my critics made me question my decision to write "Caitlin (formerly Bruce) Jenner" in my paper. I ended up asking *Hypatia* to remove "(formerly Bruce)" from my article. I now regret this decision. Presumably, deadnaming is objectionable either because it (1) *outs* a trans person; or (2) *actively calls* a trans person by their non-preferred (i.e., 'dead') name against their wishes. I did neither, but I requested the change anyway because shame distorted my judgment.

THE TURNING POINT

I owe a huge debt of gratitude to three feminist philosophers who stood by and publicly defended me despite the personal and professional costs of doing so. My graduate advisor, Kelly Oliver, quickly jumped into the fray on Facebook, bravely battling it out with bullies. She was denounced for daring to suggest that *Hypatia* host a forum of critical replies to my article. She was also bullied by philosophy graduate students at Vanderbilt, where she had worked for over a decade. Kelly was harassed so viciously that she ultimately decided to retire. She also published two pieces in my defense, one in the philosophy opinion section of the *New York Times*, and another in the *Philosophical Salon* entitled "If this is feminism . . ." Unlike my other supposed feminist mentors, Kelly knew that retracting a published article would be *bad*—not good—for my career. She was adamant throughout that I do not retract my article.

Feminist philosopher Chloë Taylor, who taught me when she was a postdoctoral student at McGill University, where I completed my undergraduate degree, also courageously defended me. Chloë had close relationships with almost all the Canadian feminists who publicly shamed me. Yet she bravely defended me on the *Daily Nous* philosophy blog and elsewhere, risking (and losing) close friendships in the process.

My best friend, feminist philosopher Alison Suen, courageously defended me on the *Daily Nous* in reply to a post by a prominent feminist philosopher. Alison was, at the time, a pre-tenure professor; siding with me risked alienating her from feminists in positions of power.

All three feminists expended a great deal of emotional energy talking to me for many hours on the phone as I broke down. If it had not been for them, and *Hypatia*'s chief editor, Sally Scholz, I would have probably retracted my article and left academia.

As it turned out, the storm passed quickly. My department colleagues at Rhodes College gave me their "complete and unconditional support." My students sent heartening emails. Within a week, a slew of supportive posts and articles were published in my defense. Brian Leiter, of the *Leiter Reports* philosophy blog, posted constant updates on the debacle and offered to raise money for legal fees should I wish to sue the journal for defamation. Justin Weinberg, of the *Daily Nous* philosophy blog, ably demonstrated that each of the complaints in the Open Letter rested on a misleading or false characterization of what I wrote. Journalist Jesse Singal soon followed suit with a damning takedown of my shamers in a *New York Magazine* piece entitled "This is What a Modern-Day Witch Hunt Looks Like." Supportive pieces were published in the *New York Times*, *The Wall Street Journal*, *The National Post*, *The Chronicle of Higher Education*, and *Inside Higher Ed*. A brave editor at the journal *Philosophy Today* volunteered to host a collection of replies to my article. A loud chorus of support quickly drowned out the sounds of the initial backlash.

Over a thousand people emailed me with supportive remarks. One was the first person in America to be legally declared non-binary. Another was the actor Paul Giamatti. Another emailer was brutally shamed online after receiving a short jail sentence for accidentally killing a biker. The rest ranged from philosophers, including many feminist philosophers, to academics in other fields, to colleagues and alumni, to everyday people. Among them were transgender people, black people, and even a couple of transracial-identified people.

I also received an email of support from Peter Singer, arguably the most famous contemporary philosopher, whose work in animal ethics I had long admired. "I see that you have been subjected to ad hominem attacks and hate mail from people who have not read, or certainly not read carefully, what you have written," he wrote. "Having been in that position myself on several occasions, I'm writing to express my regret that this has happened to you, and to encourage you to stand up for the core philosophical value of defending what you see as sound argument. Change your views when you find that there are objections you cannot meet, but not because someone abuses you. The storm will pass, but arguments endure and contribute to further useful debate." Partly in response to the *Hypatia* affair, Singer co-founded *The Journal of Controversial Ideas*, where authors can publish under a pseudonym to protect against threats to their careers or personal safety.

A TRANSFORMATIVE EXPERIENCE

In her book *Transformative Experience*, philosopher Laurie Paul explains that a transformative experience teaches you something you could not have known before going through it. No matter how much you read on the subject, you can't know "what it's like" to be a parent, fall in love, undergo a gender transition, or experience the death of a loved one prior to the experience itself. Being publicly shamed was a transformative experience for me. Sure, I could read Jon Ronson's book, *So You've Been Publicly Shamed*, meditate on the nature of shame versus guilt, and try to imagine how I'd react to a public shaming. But I had to go through one to know what it's like.

Thanks to the *Hypatia* affair, I'm a much stronger, braver, and more resilient person than I once was. I'm a more careful philosopher. Like many people, but especially women, who are taught to people-please, I was overly concerned about others' opinions. I was insecure, especially as a philosopher. I sought validation from those I respected. This anxious tendency makes for bad philosophy. It leads you to focus less on the strength of the arguments themselves and more on whether your view will please the "right" people. My experience helped free me from such anti-philosophical distractions. I no longer care if my arguments deviate from the "common" line, which may or may not be true or just. I care if they are cogent.

While public shamings threaten to undermine your better judgment, going through one *can* bring a certain kind of clarity. I now put less stock in whatever targets say or apologize for during the height of an online shaming; their judgment is too likely to be impaired. I can more easily stand my ground when people in power pressure me into silencing academic speech, such as when people on my campus pressured me to cancel a webinar I co-organized featuring Peter Singer on pandemic ethics.

When I see others being publicly shamed, I email support and advise them to step away from their computers—which I regret not doing myself. I apologize for my own mistakes, as I did upon learning that I had embarrassingly signed some petition against the philosopher Brian Leiter when I was a graduate student. I doubt that I read whatever I signed. I suppose I thought I knew all I needed to know: Leiter was "bad" in the feminist world I was part of. The irony is that while so many "feminists" were busy piling onto a junior woman in philosophy, Leiter's support of me was loud and unwavering.

CONCLUSION

A few years ago, I was asked to give a Zoom talk on the *Hypatia* affair and cancel culture in academia on my campus. During the Q&A, a frustrated student objected that I was *not* canceled. My article wasn't retracted, and I didn't lose my job. Sure, there are a few conferences where I'm not welcome, a philosopher here or there who won't be on a panel or show up to an event with me, the occasional publication opportunity extended and then retracted, potential lost professional opportunities, and a years-long hiatus from writing much of anything in philosophy but especially on this topic. But the student had a point—I didn't suffer the most severe consequences that too often accompany academic cancellations. In fact, the *Hypatia* affair provided me with numerous professional opportunities and a cherished close-knit community of friends in philosophy.

As I acknowledge how relatively "easy" I got off from this controversy, the condescending voices return. Shame for being shamed. The voices return: "Did you read Tuvel's pathetic piece on public shaming? Benatar might want to rename his volume from *Living with Adversity* to *Living with*

Huge Amounts of Privilege! How infuriating! Can you imagine philosophers rallying around a trans philosopher that way!?!!"

They have a point—and they miss the point. I am and have been incredibly fortunate. But suffering and good fortune are not mutually exclusive. Public shaming exacts a psychic and professional toll whether or not it ends in total devastation. Most who are publicly shamed do not land on their feet. They bear the full weight of the humiliation and excommunication without any of the redemptive turns I happened to experience.

The harm, moreover, does not stop at the individual. The damaging impact of cancellation efforts extends outward: even failed campaigns leave behind a chilling effect, silencing others and legitimizing tactics that corrode intellectual discourse. Some of the saddest emails I received were from early-career philosophers who abandoned projects on gender or race in the wake of the *Hypatia* affair. Other casualties of academic cancel culture include quality articles that never see the light of day due to risk-averse or politically partisan reviewers, academic minds so terrified that they choose not to research, let alone teach, controversial ideas, and generations of university students shielded from scores of dissenting perspectives.

In short, while the *Hypatia* affair ended positively for me, shame sticks to you. Hell—it took me seven years to open and read my "Hypatia ordeal" folder. And while I'm sure there's plenty here that you, dear readers, may judge or even shame me for, that's okay. I can handle it.

17

Living with one's child's Suicide

LYNNE KEETON

NEVER IN MY LIFE did I imagine I would need to learn to live with the loss to suicide of my beloved twenty-two-year-old daughter, Ceallagh. Like many journeys in life you cannot imagine how it feels on so many levels until you walk in those shoes, and it is obviously not something you would ever wish on anyone.

My very normal, cheerful, athletic, popular, primary school daughter sailed along merrily until her teens, when she started to struggle with anxiety, an eating disorder, Obsessive Compulsive Disorder (OCD), insomnia, and unrecognized depression. The wheels fell off in first year university, when it became apparent she wasn't coping. As a result, we were happy for her to take leave of absence and work on healing herself.

The next years were very up and down, but with a psychiatrist and therapist she liked and trusted, we were hopeful she was stabilizing. She was studying psychology and English, and au pairing to contribute to her income. At the age of twenty she was diagnosed as bipolar, and in the last year a form of rapid cycling which is very hard to live with and has a high suicide rate. The last six months, when she felt she was unravelling, I am grateful to have dropped what I was doing to rush to her aid. Those times we spoke gave me some insight, although I never ever imagined she would act on her thoughts. She told me "I feel I am being held hostage in this life, as I know the pain it will cause if I leave."

She seemingly was on an ideal journey with a cottage of her own near us, her beloved rescue dogs with her, and a successful application to do a BA LLB at the University of Cape Town. However, on 31 December 2019 I found her lifeless after she had taken her life by partial hanging, supposedly a peaceful way to go.

I have spent time reflecting on how I have dealt with this past two-and-a-half-year journey. I need to start with what has become a deep realization: "I was born *lucky*." I realize that on so many levels, I am so lucky to have been dealt a positive deck of cards. More specifically, I have been given a naturally resilient, positive personality.

I recognized this about myself after being attacked and raped on South Africa's Wild Coast at the age of twenty-four. Being determined to not let it ruin my life if I got out alive, I managed to go on with life relatively unscathed. I never had to dig myself out of a deep dark hole. I never worked on myself, I was just lucky. Because I never trained myself to be this way, I cannot pat myself on my back for being this way.

However, having the personality I do, has helped me navigate the dreadful road since my daughter's suicide, while still being able to experience the joy and beauty of life. However, I have cried a lot when contemplating why others, my daughter among them, are so unlucky in having mental health and other problems.

The first weeks after her death are a blur of pain, loss, regret, people, talking, and crying. Ensuring that her memorial service was a tribute to her and an opportunity to help others understand actually what this beautiful young, seemingly confident, successful girl was actually living with, was important to me. I had all my siblings from around the world for support and to help with all the practicalities.

The hardest part of the journey is the ongoing deep regrets. How my mind wishes over and over that I had hugged her more in those last weeks, that I had told her I loved her the last time I saw her, that I hadn't tried to enforce some boundaries, that I had seen better her struggle and pain, that I had learnt more about her illness . . . on and on, realizing that you cannot go back and fix any of it. Especially in that first year, whenever my mind was not occupied, it would return to that. So many regrets!

The other obvious hard part is dealing with the image of finding my daughter lifeless. I am so grateful that she looked peaceful and was not swinging from a rafter or had shot off her face. I am grateful that I, rather than somebody else, found her. My heart was so sore that when caring people spoke to me, I would dissolve in tears. The grief is something I had never experienced or imagined. It just seemed to well up from deep inside, and spill out through my eyes.

As an anesthetist, I realized I had to be able to function fully at work. Thus, I took five weeks off, allowing me time to read, weep, and to process. My colleagues were very supportive and understood that I needed to just focus on the job, but then at the end of the day were caring enough to check in on me.

An unexpected huge source of help, which I would never have imagined, came from joining an international Facebook page called "Parents who have lost a child to suicide." Losing a child is bad enough, but the loss to suicide comes with a whole lot of other issues: "what ifs?," "whys?," and guilt. It has been a massive help to be part of a community of people who fully realize the pain, and from whom I learnt many helpful tips. For example, on the first birthday without her, I decided to do something positive in her memory to make it a positive day. Ceallagh was an animal lover, and thus I collected goods and money in support of animal welfare. On that 16 October, it did help hugely to get up and do something positive in her memory, to drive out to the clinic we have been involved in, and to donate in her memory.

However, it is tragic to see daily additions to the Facebook group—parents of children as young as eleven. Those parents had no idea their children were struggling at all. Although I never ever imagined Ceallagh taking her own life, I at least had some insight.

From time to time, I felt the need to post my feelings, struggles, journey, and memories of Ceallagh on my open Facebook page. When I examined why and how it helped me, I realized it made me feel I was keeping her memory alive. I felt that wherever she may be, if she was in anyway able to see life in this world, she would be able to see the enormity of my love for her, the huge gap she has left in my life, and how much I miss her. I also have many friends around the world and their love and support made a big difference to me.

Weird as it is, extreme lockdown came a little over two months after her death, and was a good thing for me. It allowed me a lot of time to read, listen to podcasts and to think about her writings about suicide, and about being bipolar. I came to fully understand that suicide is about ending the pain of life. A quote I recently read, sums it up: "I sacrificed my life for the peace I could not find on earth." I better understood the day-to-day struggle she was living with, in spite of the daily brave face she put on.

An "app" called "The Mighty," written by people with mental health issues, has helped me increasingly understand what she was actually living with on a day-to-day basis. I just get up and live life. I don't have to consciously try and manage anxiety, OCD, sleeplessness, eating patterns, and much more, in order to stay in control and on top of life! I deeply wish I had had that knowledge while she was here. Wishing I had understood more is one of my big regrets, but I do acknowledge that I did my best, and am lucky to feel that I can't think of anything else I could have done to help her.

I did try therapy for a few weeks, mostly to cope with the flashbacks of finding her and to deal with the regrets of the last weeks. I didn't really find it helpful and realized that I am lucky to have good friends and close family to whom I can talk and with whom I can cry.

Apple Support helped me unlock her phone, for which I am grateful. It never revealed anything shocking or unknown, but it did give me better insights and left me with many precious photos and videos.

Watching videos is an especially weird and now less painful experience, as it is wonderful to see the good, funny and happy times. However, they are so alive and real that it feels so hard to accept the reality that she is gone forever. It feels scary to feel that the connections to her, and clear memories, are moving further and further away.

For me, ongoing strong connections to her are her three beloved rescue huskies. In fact, recently one was very ill and I was surprised at what a "basket case" I became, until I realised that she was the one I most associated with Ceallagh, and losing her was going to be very painful.

Ceallagh had a lot of well concealed tattoos and I went for some with her. It is a special ongoing connection I have to her and have subsequently had ones strongly linked to her added, including her ID number, which I felt the need to do soon after her death. Somehow it makes me feel linked to her.

I have a memorial bench near where I live, where she walked a lot with her dogs, where I walked with her, and where I now go often with her dogs. It is a time I allow my thoughts to go round and round over her. I have music playlists she sent me, and I walk listening to those, as they bring back strong memories.

A month or two after the COVID-19 lockdown was relaxed, I started walking again with friends, riding our horse, and bodyboarding with friends. I realise, looking back, how these fun experiences distracted me from thoughts of loss and sadness, and thus gave me mental relief and recovery time. I am very blessed to have those friends who were there for me.

As I have been fortunate, in this day and age, not to feel ashamed about this sad event in our family, and have been very open about talking and sharing my feelings, people know my journey. (I feel I am partly defined as the mother whose daughter took her own life. Sometimes my own mind screams at me: "My daughter killed herself!") I have been asked to speak to others on the same journey. I am no expert, but do know it helps to talk to someone who understands your situation from first-hand experience. Sadly, a very close friend of mine lost her son to suicide ten years ago, and has been there for me solidly. I have a new close friend who lost her daughter eight months after mine. I was asked to connect with her, and she has become a close friend.

What has been amazing are the occasional people, whom I never knew very well, stepping forward and adding to my life in ways I would never have imagined.

Obviously, Ceallagh's death has taken its toll on our family. What is hard for me is that, although I accept that people grieve differently, my husband will not talk about her at all. He says "it is tragic," "it has happened and we can't change it," and "I am not letting it destroy my life." I am not angry at him as it's his way of coping, but he is the one person I would like to be able to cry, laugh and commiserate with, as she was our child. I too am not letting it destroy my life, but she is my daughter and I do not wish to forget her. We have many good memories and photos which I wish I could share with him. It is something I just have to learn to live with . . . like her absence.

Ceallagh has a sister twenty-two months younger, who has had to manage the loss of her sister in her own difficult way. I have tried to be conscious of not making her feel that as the remaining child, she needs to feel worried about, and thus look after her mother. I need to be present for her and not let the death of her sister overshadow her life.

What has arisen and left confusion in my mind, is not knowing what there is after this life. I was raised by a very honorable, practising Christian father, and that was my belief system. I still believe in a greater power, but wish I could believe implicitly that I would see her again, and that she now exists in a place of peace, and free of pain. I do know her struggle is over. This uncertainty has led me to listen to "near death experiences," personalities who very credibly seem to have communicated with those who have left this world. Looking for conciliation, I guess, I consulted with a woman who after listening to her through many tears, did leave me feeling Ceallagh was in a better place. The other day I was thinking, "would I want her back at all costs?" and realized that I would absolutely want her back in a calm, peaceful happy life, but not back to continue her difficult ongoing painful struggle in life.

A few years after her death, I feel I miss Ceallagh more and more. I have never felt angry at the chaos and pain she wrought in our family, as I have come to deeply understand how difficult her day-today life was, with no end in sight.

Once again, I can only say how grateful I am to have been born *lucky*. To have been blessed with a stable, naturally positive personality. Although I still experience deep sorrow and waves of grief, I am able to live my life with joy. I almost feel guilty when I am told "you are so amazing to be dealing with your loss so well." I am just lucky on so many levels and eternally grateful for my blessings . . . in spite of this very painful loss of my beloved child.

18

Swimming Against Adversity

Anthony S. Rebuck

Bonnie Tsui's beautiful book, *Why We Swim*, explains that we do it for pleasure, exercise and healing. Aside from these reasons, I have used swimming twice in my life to overcome adversity.

In the 1950s, I was sent to an *almost* great English public school as a boarder—a sentence I served for six years. The school, established in the time of King Henry the Eighth, had over the years produced a number of extremely famous and successful graduates, both in literature and sport. It is unclear to me how long the culture of antisemitism had prevailed, but it was ubiquitous and thriving during my time there.

Among the several hundred students, only five of us were Jewish, and being a poor scholar, skinny and clumsy, I regarded myself (and I assumed that this was a popular opinion) as having no redeeming features. Actually, I had one. As a boy of thirteen, I possessed quite a lovely soprano voice and was welcomed into the Glee Club as a soloist. Then my voice broke, and my dulcet tones morphed into a gravelly croak.

I realized that sport might be a way to combat the incessant anti-Jewish behavior, but I was too frail for rugby, too clumsy to be a cricket star, and hopeless at running. Maybe I could be a good swimmer.

During the next summer holidays back in London, I swam every day. A famous coach at the pool saw me one day and took me under his wing.

I began to feel like some insect emerging from its chrysalis. As the weeks went by, I found that I could swim farther and faster than the other boys at the pool and people started to comment on my "nice style." The most startling change, however, was in the shape of my body; no longer skinny and droopy, I had filled out, muscles were visible for the first time, and my shoulders had expanded, literally by inches.

After the holidays, having returned to school, the swimming coach noticed me during a recreational session in the pool and asked me to stay behind for a time trial after everyone had left. Suffice to say, he told me that I would be on the senior swim team even though I was only fourteen, and should attend the team practice at midday next Sunday.

Sure enough, I turned up and was surprised to find the entire pool to myself. At lunch I asked why nobody had attended the team meeting. "You don't expect us to swim in water where a Jew-boy has been," was the reply!

To cut a long story short, I soon broke all the school swimming records, we beat all our rival schools in competitions, and I was made captain of the school swimming team. The antisemitic jibes quickly melted away.

Swimming again became my weapon against adversity about six decades later. Over the years, I had become rather fanatical about sport: running marathons, cycling, sailing and the gym, but I never swam a single stroke competitively. Then, one day in 2013, I felt a lump in my neck. The usual horror story of multiple surgeries, radiotherapy and chemotherapy ensued, and I was a mere cachectic shadow of my previous self. At the time of my five-year follow-up, I was able to engage in mild exercise on a treadmill and stationary cycle, but I was unable to lift my right arm and had difficulty with balance. The oncologist asked if I could swim and I responded that although I had been fairly good as a schoolboy, I hadn't done anything other than family swims and a little bodysurfing since. "Time to start again," he said.

My wife and I were living in Melbourne at the time, and I joined the local Masters Swimming Club. I started as the slowest swimmer in the group, but gradually, my arm strengthened, my form improved and that old pleasure of weightlessness and being at one with the water that Bonnie Tsui referred to, returned. A few very friendly, high-ranking world-record holders become my mentors and I perfected my stroke enough that these lovely old chaps put me in a relay with them at the national championships. My first gold medal!

That was the incentive for me to get professional coaching, both in Australia and in Canada. The four years since then have been an absolute thrill for me as I became National Champion, placed second in the U.S. nationals and sixth in the recent Masters World Championships in Japan!

Having cancer was an adversity, as was being weak, tired and a bag of bones. Swimming overcame all of that.

Bibliography

Becker, Ernest. *The Denial of Death*. New York: Free Press, 1973.
Benatar, David. *Better Never to Have Been*. Oxford: Oxford University Press, 2006.
———. *The Human Predicament*. New York: Oxford University Press, 2017.
———. *The Second Sexism: Discrimination Against Men and Boys*. Malden MA: Wiley-Blackwell, 2012.
Benatar, David, and David Wasserman. *Debating Procreation*. New York: Oxford University Press, 2015.
Estrich, Susan. *Real Rape*. Cambridge MA: Harvard University Press, 1987.
McCourt, Frank. *Angela's Ashes*. New York: Scribner, 1996.
Rakoff, Ruth. *When My World Was Small*, Toronto: Random House Canada, 2010.
Sheff, Nic. *Tweak: Growing Up on Methamphetamines*, New York: Atheneum, 2007.
Solomon, Andrew. *The Noonday Demon: An Atlas of Depression*, New York: Scribner, 2001.
Styron, William. *Darkness Visible: A Memoir of Madness*. New York: Random House, 1990.
Walls, Jeannette. *The Class Castle*. New York: Scribner, 2005.
Wikipedia. "Debbie Downer." https://en.wikipedia.org/wiki/Debbie_Downer.

www.ingramcontent.com/pod-product-compliance
Lightning Source LLC
Chambersburg PA
CBHW050822160426
43192CB00010B/1856